TALKING ABOUT U

GW00871603

*Six interchurch discussion booklets based on ɑ
conversations worldwide*

BOOKLET SIX

Holy Communion: the seal of unity

G. R. Evans

THE CANTERBURY PRESS NORWICH

*The Canterbury Press Norwich, St Mary's Works,
St Mary's Plain, Norwich, Norfolk NR3 3BH*

*The Canterbury Press Norwich is a publishing imprint
of Hymns Ancient & Modern Limited*

ISBN 0 907547 62 1

First published 1986

© G. R. Evans

Printed in Great Britain at the
University Press, Cambridge

A booklist

Christian communities have lately been talking to one another on several fronts. You can find an account of the way these dialogues began and a summary of what they have achieved so far in *Anglicans in Dialogue* (Church of England Board for Mission and Unity, 1984), and of others in *Growth in Unity* (see below).

Abbreviations used in these booklets

BEM	*Baptism, Eucharist and Ministry*. Faith and Order Paper 111. World Council of Churches, 1982.
ARCIC	*The Final Report of the Anglican–Roman Catholic International Commission*. SPCK/CTS, 1982.
AL	*Anglican–Lutheran Dialogue: the Report of the European Commission*. SPCK, 1983.
AR	*God's Reign and Our Unity: the Report of the Anglican–Reformed International Commission*. SPCK/St Andrew Press, 1984.
AO	*Anglican–Orthodox Dialogue: the Dublin Agreed Statement, 1984*. SPCK, 1984.
Resp.	*Towards a Church of England Response to BEM and ARCIC*. CIO, 1985.

You can buy a collection of *Reports and Agreed Statements of Ecumenical Conversations on a World Level*, ed. H. Meyer and L. Vischer (World Council of Churches, Geneva, 1984), called *Growth in Unity*.

The Bookshop, Church House, Dean's Yard, Westminster, London SW1P 3NZ, can supply all these by post, or your local bookshop can get them for you if you want to read the Reports for yourself.

Some study-guides

In the Grove Liturgical Series:

Lloyd, T. *Lay Presidency at the Eucharist* (no. 9).

Hanson, R. P. C. *Eucharistic Offering in the Early Church* (no. 19).

Buchanan, C. (ed.) *The Development of the New Eucharistic Prayers of the Church of England* (no. 20).

Cuming, G. *He Gave Thanks: An Introduction to the Eucharistic Prayer* (no. 28).

Spinks, B. *Luther's Liturgical Criteria and his Reform of the Canon of the Mass* (no. 30)

Williams, R. *Eucharistic Sacrifice – the Roots of a Metaphor* (no. 31).

The Eucharistic Liturgy: Liturgical Expression of Convergence in Faith achieved in Baptism, Eucharist and Ministry, British Council of Churches. (Referred to in this booklet as EL.)

The *Eucharistic Liturgy* was prepared for use in the full sessions of the Faith and Order Commission in Lima. It was used there in 1982 and in Geneva later in the same year at the meeting of the Central Committee of the World Council of Churches.

It has no 'authority' but that of having been used ecumenically in this way. Its contents reflect the achievement of the BEM document and it is quoted here to illustrate some of the ways in which the central questions are being answered by ecumenical endeavour.

4

6. Holy Communion: the seal of unity

The Eucharist (i.e. Thanksgiving) is a celebration

What celebration has meant most to you in your own life?

Was it the company? The significance of the event? Or something else which made it vivid and memorable and important?

At Holy Communion we are celebrating with Christ himself and with the whole company of our friends, and we are celebrating the whole life and death and resurrection and ascension of Christ and the way he has transformed our lives.

The life of Jesus was both a pure and free offering

and a victory over sin,

and through the work of the Holy Spirit it takes effect on the whole human situation.

For the first Christians the death of Jesus, his gift of himself, his resurrection which promised them a new life, were inseparable from the sense they had of being set free from sin to enjoy a new fellowship with God.

In the Eucharist we still assemble as the body of Christ, the risen Head, and celebrate through and in him what he did for us and its effect.

So the Lord's Supper is the central and unifying act of Christian worship. It brings together the two senses of the word 'communion' (*koinonia*) in the New Testament. In 1 Corinthians 10. 16 it means 'participation in the body of Christ'. In 1 John 1. 3 we find it being used for 'fellowship' ('So that you may have fellowship with us').

This double union takes place every time your own local church celebrates the Eucharist, and it is a union which includes all Christians everywhere and at all times.

Eucharistic celebrations have always to do with the whole Church, and the whole Church is involved in each local eucharistic celebration.

BEM, Eucharist, 19

In each local eucharistic celebration the visible unity and catholicity of the Church is fully manifested.

AO, 109

6

The inclusion of Christians of all ages is important, because the Eucharist is 'the meal of the Kingdom', the meal we shall all share for eternity, when time no longer divides us from those born before or after our own day.

In the eucharist we are united with one another and with all the company of heaven.

Resp. 78

The presence of the Spirit is the foretaste, pledge and first-fruits of God's coming Kingdom. At every Eucharist the Church looks forward to the consummation of that reign.

AR, 69

How is the Eucharist 'Trinitarian'?

The Eucharist involves three things:
(1) Thanksgiving to the Father.
(2) A memorial of the Son.
(3) Invocation of the Holy Spirit.

A principal source of strength in the BEM text is the central and longest section which sets forth the meaning of the Eucharist in relation to the doctrines of the Trinity (as thanksgiving to the Father, as memorial of Christ, and as invocation of the Spirit), of the Church and of eschatology

Resp. 57

The relation of the Spirit to the Father and the Son, the mutual indwelling of the persons of the Trinity, is never separated from the entire eucharistic action.

Resp. 68

(1) *Thanksgiving to the Father*

Let us give thanks to the Lord our God.
It is right to give him thanks and praise.

Truly it is right and good to glorify you,
at all times and in all places,
to offer you our thanksgiving O Lord, Holy Father,
*   Almighty and Everlasting God.*
Through your living Word you created all things,
and pronounced them good.
You made human beings in your own image,
to share your life and reflect your glory.
When the time had fully come, you gave Christ to us...
Wherefore, Lord, with the angels and all the saints,
we proclaim and sing your glory:
*   Holy, holy, holy Lord,*
*   God of power and might,*
*   Heaven and earth are full of your glory.*
*   Hosanna in the highest.*

EL

In the order of service you use in your own church you will find a version of this prayer. The Eucharist is the gift of God, but it is also man's active response to that gift in receiving it and in giving thanks for it. So the Eucharist is offered to the Father by the whole Christ, Head and members, in the power of the Spirit.

There is a two-way movement of giving and receiving. God comes to man and man comes to God.

The sacramental body and blood of the Saviour are present as an offering to the believer awaiting his welcome. When this offering is met by faith, a lifegiving encounter results.

ARCIC, Eucharist, 8

(2) *A memorial of the Son*

Memorial and sacrifice

I sacrificed my day off to help on the outing.
I sacrificed the best years of my life for you.
He sacrificed his life to save his brother from
    drowning.

We use the word 'sacrifice' to mean giving something up for someone else's sake. It can be painful even when it is a small sacrifice, like giving up a day off. In fact, if it is not painful, it is not really a sacrifice.

When we speak of the sacrifice Christ made for us, it is easy to forget the reality of the pain and the loss because the words are so familiar. We do not see the blood and agony.

9

When they tried to explain what had happened in the death and resurrection of Christ, the authors of the book and letters which are now collected together into the New Testament used pictures and imagery which were familiar to them from the Jewish Old Testament. The real bloodiness of sacrifice was a common sight in the ancient world, and their descriptions are full of it. They say that:

Jesus is the lamb sacrificed at the Passover (1 Corinthians 5. 7; 1 Peter 1. 19), a pure and perfect offering pleasing to God, the best the people could give him.

Jesus is the sin offering of the Day of Atonement (Hebrews 9. 25; Romans 3. 21–26). Once a year the High Priest entered the Holy of Holies with an offering which was made to cleanse the holy places and purify the people of God.

Jesus is the pure and perfect sacrifice made to begin the New Covenant or agreement (Mark 14. 24; 1 Peter 1. 2; Hebrews 9. 19).

Jesus is the scapegoat (1 Peter 2. 24). This beast was loaded with the people's sins and sent off into the desert to take them as far away as possible.

When St John says that Jesus is the Lamb of God who takes away the sins of the world (John 1. 29) he is bringing all these ideas of sacrifice together and saying that Jesus is both a pure and perfect and cleansing sacrifice, and the innocent carrier of all our sins.

Sacrifice in this new Christian sense is a two-way giving. Old Testament sacrifices were made by man to God. Here was a sacrifice God himself made at great cost to himself. It is a bond between man and God.

A scapegoat

It is a joyful response of creature to Creator, a cleaving to God in holy fellowship.

In this way something which happened once and for all in the past becomes real and effective in the present.

That is the meaning of the Greek word *anamnesis*, which we now translate as 'memorial' (ARCIC, Eucharist, Elucidation, 5).

If the *anamnesis* or memorial of the Eucharist makes Jesus' sacrifice real in the present, does that mean that it is itself a sacrifice? The sacrifice he made was once and for all, fully effective and complete and unrepeatable. When we speak of the Eucharist as a sacrifice, it must not be thought that it is in any way a repetition of the supreme sacrifice which reconciled man to God. That would suggest that that sacrifice had been incomplete and needed to be made again and again (ARCIC, Eucharist, Elucidation, 3). We entreat the merits of Christ's passion on behalf of the whole Church, and in that sense offer him. But he is our Priest who brings us to the Father. He offers himself in his people.

(3) *The invocation of the Spirit and the presence of Christ*

It is through the power of the Holy Spirit that the risen Lord is present in the whole Eucharistic celebration.

The strong emphasis [in BEM] on the power of the Holy Spirit as active in the whole eucharistic celebration witnesses, we believe, to the faith of the Church through the ages.

Resp. 68

13

The invocation of the Holy Spirit is rightly both upon the community and upon the elements of bread and wine.

Resp. 68

Presence

If you hold a reunion to celebrate something important to you which happened in the past, the presence of those who were there brings it back much more vividly. It seems real again.

How can something which happened once and for all in the past become real and effective in the present?

In what way is Jesus present with us in the Eucharist?

(1) His presence is absolutely real. It does not depend on how we feel or whether we have faith in it. He is just there (ARCIC, Eucharist, 8; BEM, Eucharist, 13).

(2) It is complete. We encounter in the Eucharist the whole of what Christ is and what he did for us.

The action of the Eucharist: what happens in the service

(1) Word and Sacrament

The Eucharist always includes the reading of the Scriptures often a sermon ('word') and the consecration

Present even if you are not looking

and sharing of the bread and wine ('sacrament') (BEM, Eucharist, 12; Resp. 58). The Gospel tells us of the word of God made flesh, so when we read it aloud in worship and preach it that is a memorial (*anamnesis*) of Christ just as the eucharistic meal is a memorial of him.

In the preaching of the word we can already share by exchanging preachers and hearing those of other denominations (Resp. 263). Has that happened in your church? What did you learn?

(2) *Confession and Forgiveness*

To come to the eucharist wholeheartedly and without reservation we need to come in penitence. We need to make a fresh commitment of ourselves to God and one another.

When we do that we are not trying to add to or perfect the self-offering of Jesus himself, but rather to let his self-offering work fully in us.

This is important if there is to be any meaning in our participation in the

universal communion in the body of Christ, a kingdom of justice, love and peace in the Holy Spirit.

BEM, Eucharist, 4; Resp. 76

That does not mean we must be perfect before we can come to communion. In the Eucharist itself we ask for forgiveness of our sins and for the sin of the whole world (Resp. 77). In the Eucharist the forgiveness of Christ's redeeming work is extended to us.

Most merciful God,
we confess we are in bondage to sin
and cannot free ourselves...
For the sake of your Son, Jesus Christ, have mercy on us.
Forgive us, renew us, and lead us

EL

The minister then says:

Almighty God
gave Jesus Christ to die for us
*   and for the sake of Christ forgives us all our sins.*
As a called and ordained minister of the Church
*   and by the authority of Jesus Christ,*
I therefore declare to you
the entire forgiveness of all your sins,
in the name of the Father, and of the Son,
and of the Holy Spirit.

EL

(3) *Intercession*

An important aspect of the two-way movement of gift and response between God and man in the eucharist is the congregation's prayer:

For the Church of God throughout all the world...
That the churches may discover again their visible unity...
That the churches may attain communion in the eucharist
around one table

That the churches may recognize each other's ministries.
For the leaders of the nations
that they may establish and defend justice and peace...
For those who suffer oppression or violence...

The prayers in the ecumenical Eucharistic Liturgy we have been quoting are directed especially towards the achievement of unity. But they also emphasise the Church's work in concern for the world.

The eucharist is the feast where the Church may recognize the signs of renewal already at work in the world, where, united with Christ in a special way, it prays for the world. The eucharist is the centre from which Christians go out renewed by the power of the Spirit to act as servants of reconciliation in a broken and divided world.

Resp. 74

All kinds of injustice, racism, separation and lack of freedom are radically challenged when we share in the body and blood of Christ. Through the eucharist the all-renewing grace of God penetrates and restores human personality and dignity.

BEM, Eucharist, 20

The action of the Eucharist: feeding the world

Intercession should not be just talk. The Eucharist by its very nature challenges us to confront the injustice and divisions in God's world as well as in the Church (Resp. 75, 153).

18

Jesus broke bread at the last supper he shared with his disciples before his crucifixion, and gave it to them saying, 'This is my body, which is given for you.' He gave them wine, telling them, 'This is my blood which is shed for you'. 'Do this, in remembrance of me,' he told them, and Christians have shared the mystery of that meal ever since.

Have you felt hungry? If you need food badly it is hard to think of anything else. You have no energy or appetite for the other things you could be doing, working, talking, playing. You cannot be properly yourself.

The same is true of other kinds of hunger – emotional, political, spiritual. If we are seriously hungry we cannot do things we should normally enjoy. We cannot be happy or of much use to anyone. We cannot be all that we might be.

Jesus spoke of this kind of hunger, a deep hunger for love and fulfilment, wholeness and salvation, which is in everyone. It is a hunger for that union with God which gives you fullness of life as nothing else can, because that is what he made you for.

Jesus offered himself as food to satisfy that hunger: 'I am the bread of life. He who comes to me will never be hungry. He who believes in me will never thirst' (John 6. 35).

When he entrusted to the Church the gift of the Eucharist, Jesus gave his followers food which would satisfy this deepest need of the human heart.

How can you become more aware of the Eucharist in your church as feeding you all in this way?

Can you use prayers and readings to bring out its connection with both the deep and lasting concerns and the small daily concerns of your life?

What ought we who are spiritually and physically well fed to do about the hungry of the world?

    Old people who live alone are hungry to belong.
    Unemployed young people are hungry for a sense of purpose.
    People in some parts of the world are hungry for justice.
    Others are hungry for food.

How can we include them in our celebration of the Eucharist?
How can we reach out to them?
You might like to start a scheme of practical help.

The action of the Eucharist: communion together

The process of growing together in faith cannot be separated from an actual growing together in life and worship: the practical side of ecumenism. We need 'to express visibly' the 'unity which' we 'are already experiencing' (Resp. pp. 56, 24).

The Archbishop of Canterbury with Archimandrite Sophrony of the
Orthodox Church

Shared worship in the Eucharist itself is the sign that
we are united. But all shared worship is 'a means by
which God draws our minds into union and makes it
possible to go forward ecumenically' (AR, 5).

How, then, are we to move forward to full communion with other Christians? This is the step towards which all ecumenical endeavour is working. Have we come yet to the point where, despite some differences of emphasis and interpretation, we can say:

Notwithstanding this difference of sentiment, we promise and agree to receive one another into the same affection and love; and for this among many other reasons: because we can find no warrant in the Word of God to make such difference of sentiment any bar to Communion at the Lord's Table in particular or to church fellowship in general.

Church covenant of 1780 between Baptists and Presbyterians, to form what is now New Road Baptist Church, Oxford

Some cautious moves have already been made, or are in process of being made. Some proposed changes in the canon law of the Church of England would make it possible for an Anglican priest to preside at a Eucharist using the rites of another Church, if his doing so was approved by the local bishop. It would also be possible for an ordained minister of another church to preside at a eucharist in a Church of England building, although that would be on the understanding that the Eucharist was deemed to be that of his own Church, not of the Church of England (Resp. 130). That is a kind of sharing, but it does not go far.

Another way of approaching unity is to celebrate the eucharist 'in common' with the consecration of one set of elements of bread and wine by ministers for the communions present, from which all communicants communicate. Or the celebration might be 'in parallel'; that is, involving the separate consecration of sets of elements of bread and wine by each of the ministers joining in, for his own people (Resp. 132). Here again there is little sign of the full and open-hearted union which is the essence of the eucharist and of which the Reports speak:

Anglicans and Lutherans...wish to stress [the] fruits [of the eucharist] in the building up of the community of the Church and in the strengthening of faith and hope and of witness and service in daily life. In the eucharist we already have a foretaste of the eternal joy of God's kingdom.

AL, 28

The Report of the Anglican–Orthodox Commission insists that there can really be no such thing as 'inter-communion'. Structures for sharing which hold back from full common participation are not really communion at all (AO, 19–20).

The Eucharist which unites us with Christ...unites us at the same time with one another and with the whole company of Christ's people in every age and place....

Participation in the Eucharist commits us to the ceaseless search for reconciliation among all for whom Christ died.

AR, 70

Problem-areas for discussion

(1) *How is Christ really present?*

The first attempts to explain how the bread and wine become the body and blood of Christ when they are consecrated by the president of the Eucharist in Christ's own words gave a rather simple, mechanical picture. When a loaf goes mouldy, it looks and smells different. Its characteristics change, but it is still the same stuff, bread. In the Eucharist, it was said, the opposite happens. The immaterial 'substance' of the bread and wine change into the body and blood of Christ (hence trans-substantiation) but their material characteristics stay the same. They still look and taste like bread and wine.

Today the Church does not try to find a way of expressing *how* Christ is present, because no parallel in the natural world can be satisfactory, or of saying exactly what happens, because it cannot be explained in that way. What matters is the *fact* of Christ's presence as a mysterious inner reality in the celebration of the

Eucharist. All Christians can agree that Christ is truly 'with us', in the outward, visible elements of bread and wine and invisibly in our hearts as we receive him through faith (AR, 66).

(2) Reservation

In some churches it is usual to keep some of the bread and wine after it has been consecrated to give to the sick, who cannot come to the service. In other churches this practice has been avoided because it was feared by some thinkers at the time of the Reformation that there was a danger of reverence turning into worship not of Christ but of the bread and wine, which would be an idolatry.

The BEM text emphasis that when the bread and wine become the sacramental signs of Christ's body and blood they 'remain so for the purpose of communion' (BEM, Eucharist, 15). When they are 'reserved' it must be solely for their 'distribution among the sick and those who are absent'. 'The best way of showing respect for the elements served in the eucharistic celebration is by their consumption, without excluding their use for communion of the sick' (BEM, Eucharist, 32). This is in accordance with Anglican practice (Resp. 141).

The General Synod believes 'that different practices regarding the keeping of bread and wine for the sick can be accepted'.
RespSG, p. 8, Resp. 72, 73

(3) *Presiding at the Eucharist*

Some churches allow lay people to act as president of the eucharist. Does the presidency require an ordained minister? You may find the booklet on *Ministry* helpful in thinking about this.

Not only do...Christian ministers...share through baptism in the priesthood of the people of God, but they are – particularly in presiding at the eucharist – representative of the whole Church in the fulfilment of its priestly vocation of self-offering to God as a living sacrifice (Romans 12: 1)....Their ministry is not an extension of the common Christian priesthood, but belongs to another realm of the gifts of the Spirit.

ARCIC, Ministry, 13

It is especially in the eucharistic celebration that the ordained ministry is the visible focus of the deep and all-embracing communion between Christ and the members of his body... It is Christ who invites to the meal and who presides at it. In most churches this presidency is signified and represented by an ordained minister.

BEM, Ministry, 14

One of the greatest practical difficulties lies in the Churches recognising one another's ministers as having authority to celebrate the eucharist. In the Lima Eucharistic Liturgy we met the phrase 'a called and ordained minister of the Church' in the Absolution. We have been looking at the question of Ministry in the pamphlet on

Ministry, and, in the pamphlet on *Authority*, at the great questions which lie behind. It is here, in the celebration of the eucharist together, that the mutual recognition of ministries is a most urgent issue. Unless all Christians recognise that he is 'called and ordained', no one has 'the authority of Jesus Christ' to preside over the common eucharist of the whole Church.

There is still some way to go in discussion and reflection and response to the work the Commissions have done so far before the problem of mutual recognition of ministries will be solved.

(4) *Should everyone who has been baptised be allowed to participate in the Eucharist, even infants and young children?*

In Eastern churches baptised infants are received with their parents at the communion. Their baptism has made them members of the Church and on that ground they are welcomed to communion. Most of the Churches of the West have preferred to admit only those who are old enough to understand what is happening and what the eucharist means (AR, 72).

What are the implications of admitting young children to the eucharist?

What are the implications of denying them access?

RELIGION
SOCIETY
IN NINETEENTH-
CENTURY IRELAND

SEAN CONNOLLY

Published by
DUNDALGAN PRESS (W. Tempest) LTD.

ISSN No. 0 790-2913

First Published 1985
Reprinted 1987
Reprinted 1994

Introduction

Of the different features which distinguish the inhabitants of contemporary Ireland from those of other parts of Western Europe, the role of religion remains one of the most notable. Levels of religious practice, amongst both Catholics and Protestants, are exceptionally high by European standards. Even more striking is the continuation of violent sectarian conflict, religiously defined if not necessarily religiously based, of a kind which the rest of Europe has long come to regard as part of its distant past.

The origins of these conditions are of course complex, extending over hundreds of years. A variety of recent studies, however, have focussed on the nineteenth century as the period in which the different elements which make up the distinctive religious pattern of contemporary Ireland assumed their modern shape. This pamphlet offers an overview of the major developments of that period. After a brief account of the size and social composition of the different religious denominations, it goes on to discuss the process of internal reform and revival seen in each of the major churches in the early and mid-nineteenth century. Next it examines the related questions of sectarian conflict and of the interaction between religion and politics. Finally it looks at changes in popular religious attitudes and practice, and in particular at the controversy surrounding the suggestion that the mid-nineteenth century saw a 'devotional revolution' among Irish Catholics. One result of this discussion is the suggestion that the religious history of nineteenth-century Ireland, though unusual, was not unique. Instead developments in Ireland can be best understood as an extreme example of trends also seen elsewhere in Europe at this time.

Like its predecessors, this pamphlet is intended primarily as a review of the current state of published research in the topics it examines. The names of authors cited or discussed appear in the text in capitals, and full details are given in the Select Bibliography. I am grateful to Mavis Bracegirdle, Dr A. C.

2 RELIGION AND SOCIETY IN NINETEENTH-CENTURY IRELAND

Hepburn, and Irene Whelan, all of whom read and commented on an earlier version of the text. I must particularly thank Dr Peter Brooke, whose detailed and thoughtful commentary saved me from a number of errors, and forced me to rethink several points. I am also grateful to Dr D. N. Hempton, who kindly allowed me to read his forthcoming article on the early growth of Irish Methodism.

THE CHURCHES AND THEIR MEMBERS

Throughout the nineteenth century the population of Ireland was unevenly divided between three major religious denominations. In 1834, in what appears to have been a reasonably reliable assessment based on the census of three years before, the Commissioners of Public Instruction calculated that 80.9 per cent of the population were Catholics, 10.7 per cent were members of the (Anglican) Church of Ireland, and 8.1 per cent were Presbyterians. The Catholic share of total population almost certainly increased slightly in the period up to 1845, as population continued to grow most rapidly in those regions, and among those social groups, in which Catholics were most numerous. After 1845, on the other hand, it was the Catholic population which suffered most severely from the effects of Famine mortality and of Famine and post-Famine emigration. The first true census of religion, taken in 1861, suggested that the number of Catholics had fallen by 30 per cent since 1834, while the number of Anglicans and Presbyterians had fallen by only 19 per cent in each case. As a result, Catholics now made up 77.7 per cent of total population, while Anglicans made up 12 per cent and Presbyterians 9 per cent. By 1901 the Catholic share of total population had declined a little further, to 74.2 per cent, while the proportion of Anglicans and of Presbyterians had risen to 13 per cent and 9.9 per cent respectively.

The members of these three principal denominations were unevenly distributed across the country. In 1861 Catholics made up a minority of the population in four Ulster counties (Antrim, Armagh, Down and Londonderry) as well as in the towns of Belfast and Carrickfergus. In two other Ulster counties (Fermanagh and Tyrone) they accounted for not much more than half the population. Elsewhere in Ireland Catholics were everywhere a substantial majority, making up 86 per cent of the population of Leinster, and more than 90 per cent in both Munster and Connacht. The Presbyterian population was heavily concentrated in Ulster, where 96 per cent of its members lived.

In the counties of Antrim and Down, and in Belfast and Carrickfergus, Presbyterians were in fact the largest single religious group, while they were also well represented in Co. Londonderry. Irish Anglicans were somewhat more dispersed. Fifty-six per cent of their total number lived in Ulster, just over a quarter in Leinster, some 12 per cent in Munster and 6 per cent in Connacht. Their area of greatest numerical strength, outside Ulster, was in Counties Dublin and Wicklow, and more particularly in the city and suburbs of Dublin itself.

There were also important social distinctions between the members of the three main denominations. In all parts of Ireland Anglicans were heavily over-represented among the landowning class, where they in fact made up the great majority of substantial proprietors. In the three southern provinces they were also heavily over-represented in the professions, and at the upper levels of financial and commercial life. In Ulster, however, the position was somewhat different. There too Anglicans made up the majority of landed proprietors, but below that level they ceded economic and social dominance to the Presbyterians. In the countryside Presbyterians held larger and more profitable farms than any other religious group, and were less likely to be found among the ranks of the landless labourers. In the towns, similarly, they were over-represented among skilled workers and in middle-class occupations. Ulster Anglicans, on the other hand, appear to have been represented at different levels of society — apart from the landed class — roughly in proportion to their total numbers. Ulster Catholics, finally, were a substantially disadvantaged group, overwhelmingly concentrated at the bottom of the social scale, among the cottiers, labourers and smallholders of the countryside and the unskilled and casual workers of the towns. The Catholic middle class was small, and its membership dominated by groups of limited prestige and wealth: publicans and butchers (both traditional Catholic preserves), general dealers, and teachers, for whom the pressures of a segregated society created a special niche. In the other three provinces there was a more substantial Catholic middle class, although Catholics were still under-represented in proportion to their total numbers. A rough estimate would be that Catholics in the early nineteenth century owned about one-third of total middle-class wealth.[1] The social distinctions between the denominations are neatly summed up in the statistics which the census commissioners collected on the link between religion and literacy. In 1861, 46 per cent of Catholics aged five years and over were unable to read or write, compared with 16 per cent of Anglicans and 11 per cent of Presbyterians. To put it another way, 92 per cent of those unable to read or write were Catholics, 5 per cent were Anglicans, and less than 3 per cent were Presbyterians.

In the early nineteenth century the three major denominations, Catholic, Anglican and Presbyterian, between them accounted for all but a very small proportion of the population. The Commissioners of Public Instruction in 1834 recorded a total of only 21,808 persons of other denominations, although this, as they noted, excluded a considerable number of Wesleyan Methodists 'who, although attending religious service in other places of worship, consider themselves to be in connection with the Established Church, and wished to be classed as members of that body'. By the end of the century, membership of the smaller Protestant sects had grown rapidly, despite the decline in total population. In 1861 there were 77,000 members of churches other than the three major denominations, and by 1901 125,000. Even this last figure, however, amounted to less than 3 per cent of the population. The Methodists, with 45,000 members in 1861 and 62,000 by 1901, accounted for fully half the combined membership of these smaller denominations. The next largest group, Congregationalists, had just over 10,000 members in 1901, the Unitarians just over 8,000 and the Baptists just over 7,000. The social composition of most of these lesser Protestant denominations remains to be properly investigated. GRIBBON's account of the Baptists suggests a complex pattern, changing over time. Initially concentrated among the middle classes of a few towns in the south and south-east, the Baptists began to recruit among small tenant farmers and wage earners in Ulster during the first half of the nineteenth century. In the 1850s and 60s they appear to have attracted members from a wider social range, but in the last quarter of the nineteenth century they once again narrowed their focus, drawing new recruits primarily from among skilled workers, while at the same time retaining a middle-class element in their membership. The Quakers, numbering only 2,731 individuals in 1901, were a more distinctive socio-economic group, concentrated in the middle and upper middle classes and in addition, as EVERSLEY has shown, maintaining a highly distinctive demographic pattern. Finally, there was the Jewish population of Ireland, which between 1861 and 1901 rose from less than 400 to almost ten times that number, of whom over half were to be found in Dublin city.

Even less significant, statistically at least, than the members of the lesser Protestant sects were those who disowned all religious labels. In 1861 a total of 146 persons described themselves as being of no religion, or else as atheists, freethinkers, deists, materialists, or in some other term implying a rejection of conventional religious belief. Even then the census commissioners were at pains to point out that of the 72 persons returned as being of 'no religion' seven 'were children under five years of age, and presumed to be unable to answer for themselves'.[2]

REFORM AND RENEWAL

The early and mid-nineteenth century was, throughout most of Western Europe, a period of religious revival. To some extent this can be explained as a shift in religious sentiment of a more or less cyclical nature: a reaction against the formal and unemotional piety which had dominated most varieties of European Christianity during the greater part of the preceding century. At the same time, as McLEOD suggests, a new emphasis on religious values can also be seen as a response to conflict and insecurity. In an age of political upheaval and unprecedented economic change, men and women of all social classes found in religion a symbol of identity, a guarantee of stability, or a consolation in the face of harsh reality. In Ireland, as elsewhere, the new spirit of religious conviction and commitment was seen in each of the major denominations.

The Church of Ireland at the beginning of the nineteenth century was a weak and ineffective organisation. Problems inevitable in an age of limited religious zeal were compounded by the church's established status. Bishops and archbishops were government nominees, and appointments at every level were enmeshed in the web of patronage and interest which extended through all areas of public life. The lower clergy, particularly in more remote districts, frequently failed to reside in the parishes for which they were responsible, either neglecting them altogether or committing them to the care of poorly paid and indifferently qualified curates. Many clergy were in fact pluralists, holding several widely separated benefices at the same time, so that residence was physically impossible. Even where ministers did reside, the area under their charge was often too large to be efficiently administered: the average benefice was made up of two parishes, and some were considerably larger. Churches were often in poor repair and one benefice in ten had in fact no church at all. Bishops too were frequently non-resident. One newly appointed prelate in 1782 casually informed a correspondent that he had taken advantage of a recent

7

parliamentary recess to 'run down' to his diocese 'and see what sort of thing I had gotten'.[3] Even where bishops did reside, their general conduct and discharge of their duties was often less than satisfactory. In 1801 William Stuart, Archbishop of Armagh, complained to the government that, of six bishops serving in his province, three were men of tolerable moral character but 'inactive and useless', while two others were men 'of acknowledged bad character'. The purpose of Stuart's letter was to object to a proposal to translate to the vacant see of Clogher George de la Poer Beresford, Bishop of Clonfert and Kilmacduagh and, according to his metropolitan designate, 'reported to be one of the most profligate men in Europe'. If such men were to be made bishops, Stuart continued on a note of near desperation, they should be kept in the southern part of the country, where there were few Protestants to be scandalised by their conduct.[4] Despite his objections, however, Beresford, a member of Ireland's most powerful political connection, was duly translated to Clogher. Coincidentally it was a successor in the same diocese who in 1822 created what was probably the most embarrassing single episode to affect the Church of Ireland during the period, when Bishop Percy Jocelyn was discovered in the upstairs room of a London public house in what a contemporary newspaper primly described as 'a situation with a private in the Foot Guards, to which we will not more minutely allude'.[5]

By the time of this incident, however, the character of the Church of Ireland had begun to change. The period between 1800 and 1830 was what D. H. AKENSON (1971) has termed 'The Era of Graceful Reform'. These years saw a general reorganisation and a tightening of ecclesiastical discipline, curbing if not eliminating the most serious abuses. The Board of First Fruits and Tenths, set up in the early eighteenth century to devote a proportion of ecclesiastical revenues to building and other essential purposes, was reorganised and its resources increased by generous parliamentary grants. Largely due to its work, the number of churches rose between 1787 and 1832 by nearly 30 per cent, while the proportion of parishes with glebe houses for the accommodation of a minister rose from 32 per cent to 59 per cent. During the same period, the total number of benefices rose by 25 per cent, reflecting the division of over-large unions of parishes. Pluralities were increasingly discouraged, and ministers came under growing pressure to reside in their parishes. Between 1806 and 1832 the proportion of resident incumbents rose from 46 per cent to 75 per cent. This general improvement in standards of conduct and perform-ance continued in the years after 1830, but from that point on internal renovation was increasingly combined with reforms imposed from without, by government and by public opinion. In AKENSON's terms, 'Graceful Reform' gave way to 'Reform by Critical Strangers'.

The movement for reform within the Church of Ireland had more than one source. BOWEN (1978) emphasises the impor-tance of evangelicalism. In Ireland, as in Great Britain, evangelicalism, a religion of personal experience based on the individual's intense conviction of his salvation through God's grace, had been growing in importance since the later eighteenth century, and there is no doubt that it played a significant part in encouraging many among both clergy and laity to adopt a more conscientious approach to religion and its duties. At the same time its influence should not be overstated. Although evangelicalism grew in strength among Irish Anglicans during the first half of the nineteenth century, AKENSON points out, 'it was not until the mid-nineteenth century that the church could safely be described as predominantly evangelical, and it was only after disestablishment [1869] that it became overwhelmingly so'. It was only in 1842 that the first avowed evangelical, James O'Brien of Ossory, was appointed to a bishopric. (Power le Poer Trench, the famous evangelical Archbishop of Tuam (1819-39) had experienced his conversion in 1816, when he was already Bishop of Elphin.) All in all, the evangelicals in the Church of Ireland are probably best seen as the extreme wing of a much wider shift in outlook among both clergy and laity in this period. Much of the practical work of reform that took place in the first half of the nineteenth century was in fact the work of what might best be described as conservative reformers, men like John Beresford, Archbishop of Armagh from 1822 until 1862, who were not by any stretch of the imagination evangelicals, but who were nevertheless deeply committed to the task of introducing higher standards within their church. In this they received important support from the government. In the first years after the Act of Union the subordination of ecclesiastical to political considerations reached a new peak, as government struggled to clear the long list of debts it had incurred in connection with the imposition of the Union on a largely reluctant Irish political establishment: of 12 episcopal appointments between 1801 and 1806, only two were not clearly settlements of political engagements. In the longer run, however, the Union and the consequent abolition of the Irish House of Lords made the political outlook of prospective Irish bishops a less important consideration, and post-Union governments appear to have been genuinely concerned to improve the overall quality of the episcopacy. Considerations of patronage and political interest did not cease to play a part in ecclesiastical appointments, but they were now more carefully weighed against the claims of merit and character. The state also contributed to the work of reform through legislative action — for example, the reorganisation of the Board of First Fruits and Tenths, and the acts of 1808 and 1824 providing for the more effective punishment of non-resident clergy. The changing attitude of government can in part be attributed to the increased concern with religious matters seen in society as a whole. In addition, this was a period when new ideas of efficiency and rationality were gaining ground in all departments of government, eroding the tolerance which had long existed for sinecures and irregularities of all kinds.

The Catholic church of the early nineteenth century suffered from problems very similar to those which affected its established rival. With a parish clergy dependent for their support on the fees paid for their services, as opposed to legally enforceable tithes, non-residence was not generally a problem. On the other hand, there were frequent complaints that priests neglected basic pastoral duties, failing to preach regularly, to provide for the religious instruction of the young, or to ensure that their parishioners fulfilled their obligatory religious duties. There were also claims that many priests extorted excessive sums from their

congregations in dues and fees, enforcing their demands, in total
defiance of ecclesiastical law, by maledictions from the altar and
the withholding of sacraments. Other complaints concerned the
personal behaviour of priests, in particular the freedom with
which they took part in the social life of the laity, riding to
hounds, drinking in company, presiding as guests of honour at
festive gatherings. A general laxity of ecclesiastical discipline
was further reflected in the frequent occurrence of damaging
and divisive internal disputes, where rival factions within a
diocese competed for positions of power and advantage, as well
as in the numerous local rebellions in which a priest suspended
or transferred by his bishop remained in forcible possession of
his parish, backed by all or a section of his congregation.

Problems of this kind may to some extent be attributed to
circumstances. During the first half of the eighteenth century,
the Catholic church had suffered intermittent but serious harass-
ment at the hands of the authorities. It was desperately short
of money, and became increasingly more so as its membership
grew larger but at the same time poorer, through a growth of
population heavily concentrated among the poorer classes.
Allowance must also be made for the isolated and backward
state of many of the areas to which the church's mission
extended. At the same time it seems reasonable to suggest that
the general laxity of internal discipline was a result, not just
of practical difficulties, but also of the same climate of limited
religious zeal which affected the Church of Ireland. If the
Catholic church of this period did not quite produce a Percy
Jocelyn, it nevertheless had its own episcopal scandals. Thus in
1775 Anthony Blake, Archbishop of Armagh, was suspended
by Rome on account of his consistent failure to reside in his
diocese. When John Butler, Bishop of Cork, succeeded unexpect-
edly to the family estates and the title Lord Dunboyne in 1786,
he promptly resigned his see and conformed to the Church of
Ireland, in order to be free to marry and provide an heir. In
other respects too the Catholic church of the eighteenth century,
despite its anomalous legal status, was managed on principles
not radically different to those which governed its established
rivals. Up to 1766 the exiled Stuarts were permitted to nominate

to all vacant Irish sees. Rights of presentation by landed families to particular parishes continued in some cases to be recognised up to the early nineteenth century. And even where formal rights of nomination were not involved, a degree of accommodation to the secular world may be seen in the ease with which well-born individuals like Blake and Butler rose to senior positions within the church.

In the Catholic church, as in the Church of Ireland, the late eighteenth and early nineteenth centuries saw the beginnings of a dramatic change in outlook. The most visible agents of change were a new generation of reforming bishops who set about the task of imposing higher standards of behaviour and performance on the lower clergy. The reforms introduced in different dioceses were broadly similar. Regular visitations enquired closely into the management of individual parishes. Priests were required to preach regularly, to make systematic provision for the religious instruction of the young, and to maintain a decent standard of display in their religious services. Their financial demands were more carefully regulated, and attempts were made to ensure that all money accumulated by priests returned to the church on their deaths. Regular retreats and theological conferences were instituted to improve morale and increase professional expertise. The regulations governing priests' personal conduct were tightened in various ways, forbidding them to hunt, to attend theatres, to drink in public. Their growing separation from the laity was symbolised by the adoption for the first time of a distinctive clerical dress. Initially such reforms took place within the framework of individual dioceses, with the extent and pace of change varying from place to place. Increasingly, however, individual efforts were supplemented by a degree of co-operation. In 1831 the bishops of the province of Leinster worked out a uniform code of ecclesiastical discipline for the whole province. In 1850 the Synod of Thurles, the first national assembly of the Irish church for almost 700 years, introduced a comprehensive and up-to-date code of ecclesiastical law, summarising and consolidating the reforms of the preceding fifty years.

The Synod of Thurles followed shortly on the return to Ireland of Paul Cullen (1803-78), the man who more than any other was to dominate the affairs of the Irish Catholic church over the next quarter century. Cullen, who was appointed Archbishop of Armagh in 1850 and transferred to Dublin two years later, had lived in Rome since 1821, and it was in terms of the supreme power of the papacy in Catholic affairs that he perceived his mission in Ireland. BOWEN (1983) presents Cullen's career in terms of a clash between two clear-cut ideologies: Ultramontanism, represented by Cullen himself, and Gallicanism, as represented both by old-fashioned bishops like Daniel Murray, Archbishop of Dublin (1823-52) and William Crolly, Archbishop of Armagh (1835-49), who were prepared to accept a degree of subservience to the state, and by a younger generation, led by John MacHale, Archbishop of Tuam (1834-1881), who sought instead to subordinate religion to the cause of Irish nationalism. To present the issue in these terms, however, is probably misleading. There is no doubt that Cullen himself had a strong commitment to the new ideology — distinguished by its political conservatism, its exaltation of papal authority, and its acceptance of a dogmatic, combatative theology — that had by the mid-nineteenth century achieved ascendancy within European Catholicism, and to which contemporaries gave the name 'Ultramontanism'. It is also true that there was such a thing as 'Gallicanism', a doctrine emphasising the right of national churches to manage their affairs with minimal interference from Rome. But Gallicanism as a politico-theological doctrine was likely to exist only in a fairly rarified intellectual atmosphere, such as the Catholic seminary of St Patrick's College, Maynooth. There the onslaught launched by Cullen did to some extent resemble a crusade against doctrinal error, with the principal heretic, George Crolly, Professor of Theology, being compelled in 1855 to retract his errors and visit Rome for a period of re-education. Yet, even in this case, as CORISH's study makes clear, the conflict had as much to do with differences on the question of the Queen's Colleges, and with Cullen's belief that Maynooth needed to be brought under tighter episcopal control, as with the theology of papal authority. The opposition which MacHale offered to the declaration in 1870 of papal infallability, a cause inevitably much favoured by Cullen, also lends some limited substance to the idea of a clash of ideologies. Outside these specific contexts, however, the idea is less useful. To describe as Gallicanism every attempt by Catholic priests or bishops to resist the authority of Rome in cases where its intrusion was against their interests, or even more to apply the term to every attempt to resist Cullen's relentless accumulation of power in his own hands, is to risk depriving the concept of meaning. It is true that while Cullen ruled in Ireland he promoted the advancement to bishoprics of men who shared his particular view of the supremacy of Roman authority. In the long term, however, the proposition that he was responsible for subordinating an independent national church to the authority of Rome appears more than a little dubious. The old-fashioned deference to the state of men like Crolly and Murray, which was Cullen's main target in his early years, was already being superseded well before his arrival by a more independent and combatative outlook. Within a few years of his death, furthermore, the Irish hierarchy, faced with the crisis of the Land War, were once again engaged in balancing pressures from Rome against the contrary demands of public opinion in Ireland. And where the two became irreconcileable — as in the case of the Pope's condemnation of the Plan of Campaign — it was domestic pressures which were to emerge as dominant.

What then was Cullen's importance in the development of nineteenth-century Irish Catholicism? Essentially it was that he continued the tightening of internal discipline which had been taking place in the decades prior to his arrival. During his years in Rome he had acted as agent for most of the Irish bishops in their dealings with the Congregation of Propaganda, which was responsible for what was technically the Irish mission. His personal contacts in the upper levels of the Vatican bureaucracy, his command of Italian and his known ideological soundness all combined to give him a major voice in the episcopal appointments made during his years in Ireland. The men he favoured were invariably those who shared his aim of bringing the discipline of the Irish church fully into line with that of European Catholicism. His candidates, significantly, were not usually parish priests, but instead academics or members of religious orders: men who might lack practical pastoral experience, but who could nevertheless be counted on to maintain a clearer vision of essential objectives than bishops promoted from the ranks. Although Cullen did not always get his way in the matter of appointments— he regarded the choice of Daniel McGettigan for Armagh in 1870 with dismay, and BOWEN notes a number of other cases in which Rome's decision was not to his taste— his influence was nevertheless sufficient to lead one critic, the bellettrist 'Father Prout', to talk of the 'Cullenisation' of Ireland. In reality, however, major cultural and social changes are rarely the work of single individuals. When Cullen sought to promote internal reform, he was continuing and extending trends which were already well established in the Irish church before his return from Rome. If this had not been so, he would almost certainly have made nothing like the impression he did, either on contemporaries or on later historians.

In so far as can be judged from existing writing, Irish Presbyterianism in the eighteenth and early nineteenth centuries did not suffer from the same problems of low morale and weak internal discipline which affected the two other major denominations. This can presumably be attributed to the self-governing character of Presbyterian ecclesiastical organisation. A system in which congregations chose their own ministers, and in which ultimate authority lay with a Synod representing all clergy equally and also a section of the laity, did more to ensure that individuals performed their duty, and that neglect or abuse of office was effectively dealt with, than the rigidly hierarchical structures of the Church of Ireland and of the Catholic church. The effects of the religious revival of the early nineteenth century are thus best seen, not in the area of ecclesiastical discipline, but rather in matters of doctrinal orthodoxy. Questions of doctrine had already given rise to divisions within the Synod of Ulster during the eighteenth century. In 1726 ministers unwilling to subscribe to the Westminster Confession of Faith, who the year before had been grouped together in the Presbytery of Antrim, were expelled. Shortly afterwards orthodox members who remained dissatisfied with the Synod's doctrinal position broke away to form the Secession Church.* Despite these departures at both ends of the ideological spectrum, however, the Synod of Ulster at the beginning of the nineteenth century continued to be divided between 'Old Light' supporters of theological orthodoxy and 'New Light' elements prepared to accept a looser definition of belief. All ministers were in theory required to subscribe to the Westminster Confession, but in practice many never did so.

It was only in the 1820s that these long-standing theological differences became a cause of major conflict. By this time attitudes on both sides had become more extreme. On the one hand evangelical doctrines had acquired considerable influence among both clergy and laity. On the other theological radicals had also become more bold in their views. In particular Unitarian or Arian doctrines, denying the traditional belief that Jesus had shared fully in the divine nature of God, were increasingly prominent in dissenting circles in both Ireland and Great Britain. In 1822 Henry Cooke, minister of Killyleagh in Co. Down, launched an attack on what he claimed were the Arian views held by members of the teaching staff at the Belfast Academical Institute, established in 1814, which was now the main academy for the training of prospective ministers. By 1827 Cooke had extended his campaign, successfully pressing for a firm declaration of Trinitarian belief by the Synod itself. The following year Cooke and his allies introduced new regulations providing for formal scrutiny of the beliefs of all future candidates for the ministry. The latitudinarian party, under Henry Montgomery, drew up a remonstrance protesting against the decision. When it was ignored, they seceded in 1829 to set up their own body, the Remonstrant Synod. In 1840 the Synod of Ulster, thus purged of its heterodox elements, came together with the Secession Synod to form the General Assembly of the

---

* The Secession Church was organised and served by ministers from Scotland. When in the 1740s the Scottish church split on the question of lay patronage, the Secession church followed it in dividing into burgher and anti-burgher factions. There was also in Ulster a small body of Reformed Presbyterians (also known as Covenanters or Cameronians). These were rigid Calvinists. The Presbyterians of the south had their own loose grouping, the Southern Association, which was non-subscribing and had close links with the Presbytery of Antrim.

Presbyterian Church in Ireland. The Remonstrants, meanwhile, had joined with the Presbytery of Antrim and the Synod of Munster to form the Non-Subscribing Presbyterian Association, although this was a much looser organisation than the General Assembly.

These theological disputes reflected wider social and cultural divisions. New Light views were stronger in the eastern part of Ulster, among urban Presbyterians and among the wealthier congregations, while Old Light views were stronger in the west of the province, among rural Presbyterians and among the less affluent. When the crucial Synod meeting of 1829, held in Lurgan, postponed consideration of the remonstrance to a special assembly to be held in Cookstown, the Remonstrants regarded this as a move by the conservatives to transfer the debate to territory favourable to themselves, and refused to attend. Some writers have suggested that the collision between New Light and Old Light also had a political dimension. In particular BARKLEY has argued that Cooke, while perfectly sincere in his opposition to Arianism, was primarily motivated by a belief that Montgomery and his supporters held dangerously radical political views. It is certainly true that Cooke, from the early 1830s onwards, openly allied himself with the leaders of Irish Toryism, while Montgomery was a leading spokesman for Ulster Liberalism. But it would be wrong to generalise from this concerning the political significance of the wider schism within Ulster Presbyterianism. MILLER has shown that the Presbyterian clergy who supported the United Irish movement in the 1790s were in fact evenly divided between orthodox and New Light theological views. HOLMES, similarly, notes that by no means all of those who supported Cooke's anti-Arian crusade approved of his political stance. Political differences may in some cases have given an added edge to theological debates. But there seems little doubt that the main impetus behind the divisions which opened up within Ulster Presbyterianism was the rise of evangelicalism, and the resulting demand for a firmer definition of doctrinal right and wrong.

SECTARIAN CONFLICT

Large-scale violent confrontation between Catholics and Protestants was a new development of the late eighteenth century. A degree of hostility and mistrust had of course always existed. In the first half of the eighteenth century in particular, recurrent alarms concerning the possibility of invasion or domestic insurrection had kept Protestants aware of their vulnerable position as a heavily outnumbered minority. The anti-Catholic frenzy which accompanied the Whiteboy disturbances of the 1760s, culminating in the execution of the Co. Tipperary priest, Nicholas Sheehy, in 1766, testified to the continued strength of sectarian animosities in a county where Catholic landed proprietors had survived in relatively large numbers. By the 1770s and 1780s, however, there were apparent indications that traditional fears and hostilities had begun to fade. Catholic Relief Acts in 1772, 1778 and 1782 removed the principal restrictions which had been imposed on ownership of land, on the activities of bishops, priests and regular clergy, and on Catholic education. In addition landlords and, on some occasions, local authorities showed increasing willingness to give financial aid to Catholic schools and churches. To many observers, in fact, it appeared as if the sectarian passions of the seventeenth century were at last being left behind.

It was at this point that a new form of organised sectarian violence made its first appearance in Ulster. The early history of this development remains obscure. It is generally agreed that the trouble began in parts of Co. Armagh around 1784. Because the disturbances were initially both localised and confined to the lower classes, however, they attracted little attention, so that the surviving evidence is sparse as well as often partisan. The first modern attempt to reconstruct the sequence of events, by Senior, sought the origins of sectarian tension in intensified competition for land. Elsewhere in Ireland such competition produced agrarian campaigns such as those carried on by the Whiteboys of Munster and Leinster. But in south Ulster, where

Catholics and Protestants were present in more or less equal numbers, economic rivalries were translated into sectarian hostility. SENIOR's oversimplified picture of a remorselessly exploitative tenurial system, the inevitable cause of endemic conflict, has been overtaken by historical research. More important, his emphasis on land-holding as the central issue is inappropriate to Co. Armagh. Armagh in the late eighteenth century was above all a region of rural handicraft industry. In the 1780s its sales of brown linen exceeded those of any other Ulster county. MILLER (1983) has estimated that there was an average of one linen weaver per household in the county. GIBBON, while agreeing with SENIOR in seeing the causes of sectarian tension as essentially economic, bases his interpretation on a more specific (if thinly documented) analysis of the local economy. By the 1780s, he argues, Protestant weavers in Co. Armagh were experiencing a sharp decline in status, becoming employees rather than independent producers and at the same time suffering a fall in real income. Meanwhile the economic status of the county's Catholics was rising, as they increasingly found employment in the linen manufacture. The violent attacks on Catholics by Protestant 'Peep of Day Boys' can thus be seen as an attempt by proletarianised Protestant weavers to compensate for their own declining position by reasserting their traditional economic and social superiority over their Catholic neighbours. A more recent study by MILLER (1983) also gives a place to the development of the linen industry, but sees the main origins of the disturbances in the actions of that section of the landed class who during the late 1770s and early 1780s mobilised popular support, through the Volunteer movement, in order to extort concessions from the government. In doing so they fatally weakened the traditional framework of social control. The immediate consequences were more severe in Co. Armagh than elsewhere because there the expansion of the linen industry had created a large class of Protestant weavers, too humble to be admitted to the Volunteer movement, and released by their employment in linen from the restraints traditionally imposed by family and landlord. A further dimension to events in County Armagh is suggested by CULLEN, who points to the continuation into the later eighteenth century of attempts by landlords in the southern part of the county to import Portestant tenants and actively promote cultural change. Such efforts, he suggests, meant that the tensions of a frontier society persisted longer in Co. Armagh than in most other parts of Ireland.

Given the paucity of contemporary evidence, the relative merits of these different interpretations of the Armagh troubles of the 1780s remain difficult to assess. What all the more recent accounts have in common, however, is that they locate the origins of sectarian conflict firmly in circumstances peculiar to Co. Armagh. The process by which, during the 1790s, an essentially local feud was extended to the greater part of Ireland was a complex one. By the beginning of the decade, the fighting — now dominated by two well-established secret societies, the Catholic Defenders and the Protestant Peep of Day Boys — had spread across most of south Ulster. In addition the Defenders had spread into the northern half of Leinster and into parts of Connacht. Here, in the absence of a substantial body of Protestant opponents, they concerned themselves primarily with economic grievances relating to tithes, taxes, employment and the occupation of land, while at the same time retaining something of their original sectarian character. In September 1795 Protestants who had successfully beaten off a Defender attack near Loughgall, Co. Armagh, organised themselves into a new, more disciplined force, the Orange Order. By this time, sectarian conflict was increasingly becoming interlocked with the political confrontation between the government and the militant radical movement which had been inspired by the French revolution. Already in the early 1790s, some of the Defenders showed evidence of having been influenced by events in France. In the summer of 1795 the Defender leadership concluded a formal alliance with the United Irish society, now itself reorganised as a secret organisation working towards a revolution in Ireland to be carried out with French assistance. As the Defender-United Irish alliance became steadily more threatening, central and local government looked increasingly to the Orange Order as an ally against both internal disaffection and foreign invasion.

This recruitment of plebeian allies whose basic motivation was sectarian was not undertaken lightly by either side. The insistence of the United Irish leaders that an insurrection could take place only with French help was not, Elliott suggests, based solely on military grounds: in addition, middle-class radicals looked to French troops to keep the rank and file of their own movement under control, ensuring that political revolution did not turn into either a general assault on property or a religious war. The government and landed class, for their part, showed little initial enthusiasm for armed associations of lower-class Protestants. A section of the Armagh gentry supported the Orange Order from the start, but the majority continued for some time to regard it with suspicion and distaste. As the decisive confrontation approached, however, neither side could afford to be squeamish in its choice of supporters. By mid-1797 the growing power of the United Irishmen and Defenders had won the Orange Order the support of a majority of landed gentlemen, and the reluctant acceptance of the government. The United Irishmen, meanwhile, were making free use of anti-Orange propaganda in order to build up support for the revolutionary movement, not only in Ulster but also in parts of the south where Orangeism was as yet scarcely known. Of the four localised rebellions which broke out in the summer of 1798, the most formidable and prolonged, in the south-east, assumed the character of a religious civil war, in which the rebels brutally slaughtered Protestant non-combatants who fell into their hands, while the suppression of the rebellion in that region was succeeded by a reign of terror directed against Catholics. Elsewhere, in Connacht and in the counties round Dublin, religion played a smaller part, but there too occasional evidence of sectarian purpose on the part of the rebels, and the free use of Orange insignia by government forces, confirmed for both sides that religious, political and social conflicts were inextricably linked.

It is hardly surprising, in the light of these events, that a deep distrust between Catholics and Protestants, and a determination by each side to maintain its territory against the encroachments of the other, continued throughout the nineteenth century to influence all parts of Ireland and all social classes. In rural Ulster the pattern of recurrent violence established in the 1780s and 1790s continued. A new Catholic society, the Ribbonmen, succeeded the Defenders as the organised opponents of the Orange Order. To regular clashes at fairs and other meeting places was added the violence arising out of formal processions, the characteristic means by which each side sought to demonstrate its territorial supremacy and deny that of the other party. In some cases routine brawls gave way to more serious violence, as at Dolly's Brae near Castlewellan, Co. Down, where 8 people died following a Ribbon attack on an Orange procession in 1849. Sectarian fighting also spread to the towns. Belfast in the late eighteenth century had enjoyed a reputation as a centre of religious liberalism. But Catholics, at that point, had amounted to no more than 10 per cent of the town's inhabitants. The first half of the nineteenth century saw Belfast's population multiply five-fold, as expanding manufactures attracted migrants from rural Ulster. Those migrants, Catholic and Protestant alike, brought with them what were by now well-established traditions of sectarian feuding. Their presence, moreover, dramatically altered the religious composition of the town's population. By 1834 Catholics made up nearly one-third of Belfast's inhabitants; ten years later they may have accounted for over 40 per cent. Belfast's first recorded sectarian affray had taken place as early as 1813, following Orange celebrations on 12 July. There was fighting in 1832, following a Tory victory in the town's first parliamentary election, and again in 1835, 1843 and 1852, in each case arising out of 12 July celebrations. In 1857 aggressive street preaching by militant Protestant clergymen provoked Belfast's most violent sectarian riots to date. Worse still followed in 1864, when a nationalist demonstration provoked two weeks of rioting in which 11 people died. The introduction and defeat of the first Home Rule Bill in 1886 led to fighting extending over several months, in which 32 deaths were recorded and the actual number killed may well have been substantially higher.

In nineteenth-century Belfast, as in late eighteenth-century Co. Armagh, sectarian violence was above all the product of an unstable balance of denominational strength. Strong anti-Catholic feeling among Belfast Protestants in the mid-nineteenth century reflected a real fear that if existing trends continued Belfast would become a predominantly Catholic city. By the time it became clear that this was not in fact going to happen, the threat of local engulfment had been replaced by the spectre of catastrophe at national level, in the form of Home Rule. The same theme of conflict as the result of a shifting balance of forces occurs in the case of Derry, which had its first major sectarian riots in 1870 and 1883. There too the proportion of Catholics had risen rapidly in preceding decades. In addition the railway, making possible an influx of large numbers of Protestants from outside the city for the traditional processions on 12 July and 12 August, was blamed for transforming uncontentious local festivals into occasions for violent confrontation.

Outside Ulster too, popular sectarianism remained strong, at least in the first half of the nineteenth century. DONNELLY has listed some of the factors which helped to perpetuate anti-Protestant feeling among the Catholic lower classes. All three of the forces deployed against the recurrent agrarian disturbances of the period, the Yeomanry, the County Constabulary and the regular Army, were predominantly Protestant, and the first two were widely penetrated by Orangeism. The resentment inspired by tough and sometimes brutal policing was thus easily translated into sectarian terms. Tithes, the tax on agricultural produce levied for the support of the Church of Ireland, remained a major grievance up to 1838. Passions were further inflamed by the activities of different Protestant missionary and educational societies. Since Protestants outside Ulster nowhere amounted to more than a small proportion of the population, there was little scope for the sort of head-on sectarian clashes seen in northern districts. But popular ballads and poems, political slogans and the threatening letters that accompanied or preceded agrarian outrage all made free use of the language of religious hatred. The strength of anti-Protestant sentiment was also vividly reflected in the millenarian ideas which repeatedly surfaced among the Catholic lower classes of the south. Millenarianism, the belief in an imminent fulfillment of the prophecies of the

New Testament concerning the second coming of Christ, has existed in many different societies and at different social levels. Among the poor and powerless such ideas, holding out the prospect of a divinely-ordained overthrow of the existing social and political order, has been one classic response to conditions of upheaval, anxiety or deprivation. Thus it is not surprising that the prophecies of Pastorini, the best known millenarian writer of this period, appear to have first obtained popular currency during the typhus epidemic of 1817, and reached their widest circulation in the years of depression and threatened famine during the early 1820s. What gave the millenarianism of pre-Famine Ireland particular significance, however, was its single-minded focus on the issue of sectarian conflict. Thus the prophecies of Pastorini as understood by Irish Catholics centred round the total destruction — expected to come in 1825 — of the Protestant churches, the locusts from the bottomless pit whom the Book of Revelation had foretold would be permitted to torment the faithful for three hundred years before being annihilated. In the same way prophecies circulated in the 1840s and attributed to the medieval Irish saint Colmcille predicted a general massacre of the Catholics of Ulster, organised by the Protestant clergy of the province, after which a league of Catholic nations would intervene to stamp out heresy in both Ireland and Great Britain. The real influence of ideas of this kind is of course difficult to assess. But DONNELLY has argued that the prophecies of Pastorini played an important part in giving the Rockite disturbances of the early 1820s a confidence and a base in communal solidarity which made them particularly formidable.

Higher up the social scale, the tone of relations between Catholics and Protestants in the early nineteenth century varied. The events of the 1790s had undoubtedly intensified religious divisions. The revival of anti-Catholic feeling among the Protestant upper and middle classes was reflected in the popularity of works like Sir Richard Musgrave's *Memoirs of the Different Rebellions in Ireland* (1801), which presented the rebellion of 1798 as a primarily religious movement, connived at and actively encouraged by the Catholic clergy. At the same time a considerable degree of mutual tolerance and practical co-operation continued into the first two decades of the nineteenth century. Anglican and Catholic clergy attended one another's public functions, while clergy and laity of different denominations were also willing to work together in a wide range of charitable ventures. The Kildare Place Society, set up in 1811 to provide an elementary education for the common people 'divested of all sectarian divisions in Christianity', included prominent Catholics on its board of management, and received widespread support from Catholic clergy and laity. As late as 1824 James Warren Doyle, Catholic bishop of Kildare and Leighlin, argued in a public letter that it should be possible to reunite the churches of England and Rome, if men of good will would get together to examine the differences which separated them.

After 1820 three developments largely destroyed this continuing tolerance and co-operation. The first was the launching of the so-called 'Second Reformation'. One consequence of the growth of evangelicalism among the different Protestant denominations had been the appearance of a new interest in missionary efforts, directed not just at the heathen overseas but also at the Catholic population of Ireland. The first such venture came as early as 1799, when the Irish Methodists sent out three missionaries to preach to Catholic audiences. During the early decades of the nineteenth century a bewildering assortment of societies came into being, all dedicated to the same task of promoting the conversion of Ireland's Catholics. Among the more important were the Hibernian Bible Society (1806), the Irish Society for Promoting the Education of the Native Irish through the Medium of their own Language (1818) and the Scripture Readers' Society (1822). The different societies trained and supported itinerant preachers, many of them fluent speakers of Irish, distributed huge numbers of bibles and tracts and, most important of all, established schools offering an elementary education free of charge to all who were prepared to accept the religious instruction that accompanied it. They also established colonies in which converts from Catholicism could live protected from intimidation by their former co-religionists, the best known being those set up on the estate of

Lord Ventry near Dingle, Co. Kerry, and on Achill Island off the coast of Co. Mayo. In the immediate aftermath of the Famine, the Society for Irish Church Missions, founded in 1849 by the Rev. Alexander Dallas, launched a renewed campaign of proselytism in the most distressed parts of Connacht. None of these efforts achieved any lasting success. Gains made by the concentration of massive resources in areas where the population was particularly poor and the Catholic church establishment deficient did not provide the hoped-for springboard for wider expansion, and such gains themselves proved impossible to sustain in the long term. The influence of the Protestant missionary societies receded in the south-west from the late 1840s and in Connacht from the mid-1850s, the decline being hastened in each case by a determined Catholic counter attack spearheaded by the Redemptorists and other missionary orders. Despite this, the effect of the Second Reformation on relations between Catholics and Protestants was catastrophic. Clergymen who had previously been willing to work together on matters of common concern now came to regard one another as rivals and potential aggressors. The inevitable recriminations and accusations exchanged by Catholic and Protestant spokesmen, along with the frequent and sometimes violent local quarrels arising out of the activities of itinerant preachers or of evangelical education societies, created resentment and suspicion on both sides. A particularly emotive issue was the frequent charge — generally but not always groundless — that during Famine relief operations aid had been granted or withheld to induce Catholics to change their religion.

At the same time that changes within Irish and British Protestantism were producing this new and disruptive missionary zeal, Irish Catholicism was also becoming more combative in outlook. BOWEN attributes this development largely to the personal influence of Paul Cullen, whom he presents as seeking to institute 'religious apartheid' and to promote a movement for 'Catholic ascendancy' in Ireland. As with the case of internal reform, however, this focus on a single individual is misleading. Cullen's attitude to persons of other faiths was certainly a harsh one. In 1865, for example, he boasted that he had never dined with a Protestant, and commended an archaic ecclesiastical regulation which had forbidden any priest to do so. But in this he was at most an extreme example of a wider trend. By the mid-nineteenth century Catholicism throughout Europe was reacting to the challenge of an increasingly pluralist and rationalist society by a vigorous assertion of its exclusive claims to truth and authority. The Syllabus of Errors (1864), the determined defence of the pope's temporal possessions against the movement for Italian unification, and the proclamation of papal infallability (1870), were all reflections of this mood of intransigent defiance in the face of a hostile world. To Protestants, of course, all this was evidence that Catholicism had shed neither its authoritarian character nor its imperialist ambitions. In particular the restoration of the English Catholic hierarchy in 1850 provoked a wave of anti-papal and anti-Catholic hysteria in both Ireland and Great Britain.

The triumph of this aggressive outlook within Catholicism also affected denominational relations in more practical ways. Marriages between Catholics and Protestants, already regarded with disfavour by the Catholic clergy of the early nineteenth century, were now even more strongly discouraged. New regulations introduced at the Synod of Thurles in 1850 largely anticipated the notorious *Ne Temere* decree of half a century later. Protestant partners were required to give guarantees that all children would be brought up as Catholics, and the church's disapproval of the union was to be expressed in the withholding of much of the normal marriage ritual. There was also a major change in attitudes to education. In the early nineteenth century many Catholic bishops and clergy were prepared to accept a system of non-denominational schooling. Indeed Bishop Doyle of Kildare and Leighlin had in 1825 positively advocated mixed education as a means of promoting better relations between Catholics and Protestants. Although some bishops opposed the non-denominational National School system introduced in 1831, others were prepared to accept it, and their position was endorsed by Rome in 1841. Thereafter, however, attitudes hardened. On the issue of the non-denominational Queen's Colleges set up at Cork, Galway and Belfast in 1845, the bishops were evenly divided. However it was, as WHYTE, (1967) notes, a division between generations. Of 15 bishops aged over 60, 10 were prepared to accept the colleges, while of 11 bishops aged 60 and under, 8 rejected them. In the later nineteenth century, the consistent demand of the Catholic church authorities was for the consolidation of denominational education at every level from the primary school classroom to the university lecture hall. They were of course confirmed in this stance by the open use of schools for proselytising purposes by the agents of the Second Reformation. In this as in other respects, militant Protestantism and militant Catholicism, products of the same general religious revival, were also mutually reinforcing movements, each confirming the other in its vision of Ireland as a battleground in which religious truth confronted rampant error.

The third major development which from the 1820s further divided Catholics and Protestants was the emergence of a new style of popular politics. Between 1824 and 1829 middle-class leaders, headed by Daniel O'Connell, employed a range of novel techniques of mass agitation to build up popular support behind their campaign for 'Catholic Emancipation', the removal of the principal legal restrictions still affecting Catholics. A popular political movement of this kind, challenging the basic assumptions of a political system based on the deferential acceptance of rule by an elite, was in itself deeply alarming to contemporaries. But the struggle for and against emancipation was also inevitably perceived, on both sides, as a religious conflict. Recent studies of Daniel O'Connell have tended to emphasise his status as a major spokesman for European liberalism, and his strong personal commitment to civil equality and religious toleration. At the same time Ó TUATHAIGH and DONNELLY have shown the extent to which, at popular level, the emancipation campaign became the focus for many of the same resentments that had earlier found expression in agrarian violence, as well as for the mood of millenarian expectation that shortly before had made Pastorini a household name. When it became necessary to connect the two worlds of high and popular politics, furthermore, O'Connell and his colleagues were fully prepared to do so, with a rhetoric that explicitly linked religious, political and economic grievances. The fears which such proceedings inevitably aroused among Protestants were amply confirmed when the granting of Catholic demands was followed almost immediately by a direct attack on the privileges of the established church, in the shape of a campaign between 1830 and 1838 for the abolition of tithes. Like the emancipation campaign, the anti-tithe movement was an open constitutional agitation which in practice derived much of its force from the implied threat of violence. In this case, furthermore, the methods of passive resistance advocated by the Catholic leaders frequently gave way to open violence and intimidation. When after 1840 popular attention had shifted to a nominally secular issue—the campaign for repeal of the Act of Union—Irish political divisions had taken on a clear-cut religious character. Repeal was overwhelmingly a Catholic demand, bitterly opposed by the great majority of Irish Protestants. As in the 1820s and 30s, the Catholic clergy played a prominent part in the agitation, and one of the issues which eventually precipitated a split between O'Connell and some of the handful of liberal Protestants who initially supported him was O'Connell's willingness to repay this backing by throwing the weight of the Repeal movement behind such explicitly Catholic causes as the demand for denominational education.

By the middle of the nineteenth century the bloodshed and repression of the 1790s, the tensions created by the Second Reformation and the fears and passions aroused by the new style of political agitation had combined to produce a deep religious division at all social levels. Observers were struck by the extent to which the Catholic and Protestant middle classes avoided mixing socially. In parts of the south-east, it was claimed, there were not only separate Catholic and Protestant inns, but even separate Catholic and Protestant stage coaches travelling the same routes. However such reports, in the 1830s and '40s, probably reflect the high point of sectarian animosity in most parts of Ireland. With nine-tenths or more of the population belonging to the same denomination, strong sectarian feeling made sense only as long as the smaller side retained a grossly disproportionate share of power and privilege. That was very much the case in the early nineteenth century. Thereafter, however, the progressive dismantling of institutionalised Protestant privilege, culminating in the disestablishment of the Church of Ireland in 1869, removed most of the basis for serious resentment. Tensions were further reduced as the changing social composition of the Catholic population after the Famine was reflected in a more sophisticated style of popular politics. Only in Ulster did a more even denominational balance provide the basis for continued open sectarian confrontation after mid-century. Yet moderation elsewhere of the open hostility seen in earlier decades did not mean that religious tensions were forgotten. In the late nineteenth century Catholics and Protestants lived in their own social circles, supported their own educational, medical and charitable institutions, and took opposite sides in politics: no longer warring but still very much separate peoples.

THE CHURCHES AND POLITICS

Close links between Irish religion and Irish politics were hardly a new development of the nineteenth century. During that century, however, there were important changes in the nature of those links, and in the relationship between all three major religious denominations and the state.

For Irish Anglicans, the central development was the progressive loss of privilege. At the start of the nineteenth century, the Church of Ireland was still an established church. Its bishops sat in the House of Lords; its parishes were units of local government; most important, the entire agricultural population was legally obliged to contribute to its financial support. In addition, members of the Church of Ireland continued to dominate the political system, retaining a disproportionate share even of those positions of influence and profit for which the relief measures of the late eighteenth century had in theory made Catholics and Presbyterians also eligible. Already in the opening decades of the nineteenth century, however, both formal and informal privilege was coming under attack. The reasons for this lay in the general development of Irish government in the decades after the Union. A major feature of that development was the emergence of what MacDonagh (1968) terms the concept of the neutral state: the growing recognition, partly in response to the increasing political assertiveness of Irish Catholics and partly as a reflection of wider changes in political attitudes, that government in Ireland could not hope to be either effective or generally accepted as long as it remained the exclusive preserve of any single group. The most visible indication of this new outlook was the growing willingness of governments, beginning with the Whig administration of 1835-40, to distribute a reasonable share of patronage to all religious denominations. The process of change was inevitably a slow one, fluctuating with the state of Irish politics, and the social and educational advantages of Anglicans ensured that they remained at all times over-represented at the middle and

c

upper levels of government. Nevertheless, by the later nineteenth century what had been a near monopoly was now broken. The assault on the legal privileges of the Church of Ireland also began in the 1830s. The Church Temporalities Act (1833) imposed drastic reforms, reducing the number of archbishops from four to two and the number of bishops by ten, and creating a body of ecclesiastical commissioners with control of a substantial part of the Church's income. The creation in 1831 of a non-denominational system of elementary schooling was also seen by many churchmen as setting aside one of the exclusive prerogatives of an established church. On the question of tithe, the major practical grievance of opponents of the Church of Ireland, an act of 1838 offered a compromise, converting tithes into a concealed payment, set at a lower level than formerly and subsumed into the tenant's rent. With this concession, the position of the established church ceased for the moment to be a central issue. However, when pressure was renewed, by an alliance of Irish Catholics and Irish and British Nonconformists, in the 1850s and '60s, it could not be resisted. An act to abolish all state endowments of religion (including the *regium donum* paid to the Presbyterian clergy and the annual grant to Maynooth College) received the royal assent in 1869, and took effect from 1 January 1871. The terms of the disestablishment act left the Church of Ireland with a healthy financial endowment, and its members continued to include the greater part of the country's social elite. At the same time its role had been completely redefined. From being the religious embodiment of civil society, it had become the church of a socially advantaged but numerically weak minority.

Among Irish Presbyterians, the nineteenth century saw a long drawn out and complex readjustment of political allegiances. In the last quarter of the eighteenth century, the Presbyterians of Ulster had been the main power base of successive radical movements, from the Volunteers to the United Irishmen. More than 20 Presbyterian ministers took part in the Ulster rebellion of June 1798, of whom four were later executed for their activities while others were imprisoned or banished. It is hardly surprising, therefore, that in the first years after the Union

Presbyterians continued to be regarded with suspicion by the political establishment. When the government in 1803 increased the *regium donum,* at the same time classifying ministers into three groups paid at different rates, this was a conscious attempt to increase the state's control over what was seen as a potentially subversive group. Within a few years, however, it was clear that such suspicions were no longer well founded. Presbyterian political behaviour in the late eighteenth century, as STEWART and others have pointed out, had been closely determined by religious geography. Support for the United Irishmen came mainly from the Presbyterians of the overwhelmingly Protestant north-east. Elsewhere in Ulster, where Presbyterians lived side by side with a large and increasingly aggressive Catholic population, they showed far less enthusiasm for radical politics. In the counties of Fermanagh, Tyrone, Londonderry and Armagh, it was later claimed, there were 14,000 yeomen, of whom three quarters were Presbyterians and a large majority also Orangemen.[6] The Presbyterians who had responded most eagerly to the United Irishmen's call for a union of Catholics and Protestants behind common political goals, in other words, were those who did not themselves have to experience the day-to-day realities of co-existence. The events of 1798 brutally exposed the limitations of such a parochial outlook. News of sectarian massacres in the south forced Presbyterians to look beyond the security of their immediate environment and see themselves as part of a vulnerable Protestant minority in a predominantly Catholic Ireland. Already in the second half of 1798 reports from the north-east spoke of large numbers of former United Irishmen joining the yeomanry and in some cases the Orange Order. Within a few years even the most hostile observers agreed that support for revolutionary politics among Ulster Presbyterians had dwindled to insignificance.

Daniel O'Connell, speaking in 1841, summed up what has remained the most common view of the political evolution of Ulster Presbyterians in the period after 1798: 'The Presbyterians fought badly at Ballynahinch. They were commanded there by one Dickie an attorney, and as soon as the fellows were checked, they became furious Orangemen, and have continued so ever since'.[7] O'Connell's remarks were perhaps a fair reflection of the extent of religious divisions in Ireland by the early 1840s. As a summary of what had happened to Presbyterian political attitudes, however, they were a wilful over-simplification. Ulster Presbyterians abandoned revolutionary politics after 1798, but they did not thereby become 'furious Orangemen'. It is true that in 1834 Henry Cooke, the best known Presbyterian spokesman of the mid-nineteenth century, had apeared at a rally organised by the leaders of Ulster Toryism at Hillsborough, Co. Down, to proclaim what he called the banns of marriage between the Presbyterian Church and the Church of Ireland, henceforth bound together in common defence of the constitution and the union with Britain. In this, however, Cooke was far from speaking for Presbyterians as a whole. Instead, as HOLMES has shown, his increasingly open identification with Tory politics was widely criticised by other leading Presbyterians. Although many Presbyterian voters now supported Tory candidates, others continued to give their backing, through Whig and Liberal candidates, to the cause of moderate reform. Presbyterian clergymen played a prominent part in the agitation during the 1840s and 1850s for tenant right: in 1850 Cooke complained of the 'perfect Communist interpretations' advanced by some ministers. In the 1880s agrarian grievances briefly united Catholics and a substantial proportion of the Presbyterian farming population behind the Liberal party. The events of this period, as analysed by BEW and WRIGHT, are strikingly reminiscent of the 1790s. Once again Presbyterians in the west and south of Ulster abandoned the agitation at an early stage, as the agrarian campaign became increasingly tied up with the Nationalist political advance. The Presbyterian tenant farmers of the securely Protestant north-east, on the other hand, remained loyal much longer to the Liberal cause. For them it was once again a crisis at national level, the introduction of Gladstone's Home Rule Bill in 1886, that finally overcame more parochial concerns. After 1886 Ulster Presbyterians turned overwhelmingly to Conservative candidates although even then, as McMINN has shown, many continued to have reservations about thus committing themselves to the support of what they still considered an Anglican-dominated political establishment.

For the Catholic Church the nineteenth century brought a change in status the opposite of that experienced by its established counterpart. During the first decades of the nineteenth century, a cautious and even timid attitude towards government, the legacy of a long period of dependence on official toleration, gave way to an increasingly assertive defence of what were seen as Catholic interests, as well as a claim to be heard as spokesmen on a range of wider issues. The political establishment, meanwhile, began to treat Catholic priests and bishops with increasing respect. Senior ecclesiastics were invited to official functions and nominated to sit on public bodies. In 1846 Archbishop Murray was even offered a place on the Irish Privy Council. However he declined to accept it, just as his successors, Paul Cullen and Edward McCabe, consistently declined invitations to receptions at Dublin Castle. Such refusals were perhaps the most eloquent testimony to the status which the Catholic Church had achieved by mid-century: a powerful interest group, constrained in its dealings with the state only by the need to avoid alienating its own followers by seeming to establish too close a relationship.

The main use the Catholic church authorities made of their enhanced status was to press their claims in educational matters. By the middle of the nineteenth century, as was seen earlier, they were firmly committed to the principle of denominational education at all levels. Their efforts to achieve this were most successful in the case of primary schooling. The National Schools established in 1831 had been intended to provide a mixed education: in practice, most were from the start attended mainly by pupils from one particular denomination, and a high proportion were in fact managed by local clergymen. During the second half of the nineteenth century, this *de facto* denominationalism was confirmed and institutionalised. The regulations governing the provision of religious instruction during school hours were relaxed, the number of schools under clerical management and attended exclusively by members of one denomination continued to increase, and in 1883 even denominational teacher-training colleges were established. Perhaps the most revealing episode, however, had been in 1853, when Richard Whately, Anglican archbishop of Dublin, resigned from the Board of Commissioners of National Education after having been defeated in a bitter dispute over its failure to insist on the use of two books of non-denominational religious instruction published by the Board and written by Whately himself. What was significant was not just Whately's failure to carry his point with the Board but also, as AKENSON (1981) points out, the attitude of the Irish government, which stood by and allowed him to be humiliated. Where third-level education was concerned, the efforts of the Catholic church were much less effective. Here the bishops chose to take an uncompromising stand for denominationalism and nothing less, rather than, as in the case of the national schools, subverting a non-denominational system from within. This was despite the fact that their claims were weakened by the under-representation of Catholics in the social groups eligible for higher education, as well as by the reluctance of many of those so eligible to compromise their prospects of social advancement by accepting consignment to an educational ghetto. Liberal governments, constrained by Nonconformist hostility to any endowment of religious institutions, and Conservatives, unwilling to incur the hostility of Irish Protestants and their British sympathisers, proved equally unwilling to meet such a demand. The Catholic University, established in 1854 as an alternative to the Queen's Colleges, continued to be denied state support, and it was not until 1908 that the government finally endowed what was in effect a Catholic institution of higher education, the National University of Ireland.

A central feature of the new public role assumed by the Catholic clergy was their prominent involvement in secular politics. This began with the campaign for Catholic Emancipation in 1824-9, when priests throughout the country played a crucial role as local agents and organisers for the Catholic Association: publicising the agitation from their pulpits, speaking at public meetings, organising and serving on local committees, canvassing voters, heading processions of their parishioners to the polling booth to support candidates favoured by the Association. After the Catholic Relief Act, the bishops attempted to withdraw the clergy from political agitation, but with limited success. In particular, the major agitation against tithes between 1831 and 1838 kept many priests involved in public affairs. When a major agitation for repeal of the Act of Union was launched in 1840, Catholic bishops and priests once again played a prominent part at every level of the agitation. The tradition of clerical political involvement thus established continued into the second half of the nineteenth century, as priests played a central role in a succession of political movements, from the Independent Irish Party in the 1850s to the Anti-Parnellite Nationalists in the 1890s. O'SHEA, in a case study of Co. Tipperary, calculates that 77 per cent of the priests who served in the county between 1850 and 1891 took some part in politics. To see the matter from a somewhat different perspective: between 1853 and 1892 no less than 9 Irish M.P.s were unseated on the grounds that their election had involved the exercise of undue influence, in some cases constituting 'spiritual intimidation', in others physical violence, on the part of Catholic priests.

This prominent political involvement led many contemporaries to allege that it was in fact the Catholic clergy who were the real controlling force behind Irish popular politics. Historians have not generally agreed. A partial exception is Professor Emmet LARKIN, who in a series of monographs has developed the view that the Catholic church played a crucial role in the development of Irish nationalist politics during what he regards as the formative period 1878-91. Specifically he argues that it was the influence of the church which ensured that what emerged during this period was a stable political system governed by democratic rules. This, however, is a view of politics taken very much from the centre, through the correspondence of bishops, Roman officials and senior politicians. Historians who have looked instead at the practical workings of popular politics have in general come away with a more cautious assessment of the extent of clerical influence. WHYTE, in a general survey of the part played by priests in elections during the nineteenth century, concludes that their power was at its highest in the 1850s and 1860s. Thereafter, he suggests, clerical influence declined, as the expansion of the Catholic middle class made the assistance of priests less necessary, and their claims to a preponderant voice less acceptable. Even at its mid-century high point, furthermore, the priest's authority was less than contemporaries maintained. The same conclusion emerges from more detailed studies. O'FERRALL, examining the Catholic emancipation campaign, emphasises the essentially secondary role of the clergy: 'priests were generally willing and able assistants and only a few exceptional priests became full partners in local leadership with lay middle-class Catholics'. O'SHEA, discussing post-Famine Tipperary, also stresses the limits of clerical power, and the extent to which the leadership assumed by the priests depended on a substantial identity of social and economic outlook between themselves and their congregations. WOODS, examining the general election of 1892, when the Catholic clergy threw their full weight against Parnell and his supporters, finds no correlation between the intensity of clerical activity in individual constituencies and the strength of the anti-Parnellite vote.

None of this is intended to deny that the role of the priest in secular politics was an important one. It could hardly have been otherwise. The Catholic parish clergy were a body of men educated to a minimum standard, familiar with basic organisational procedures, evenly distributed across the country, and easily communicated with through the agency of their bishops. They were prominent local figures, intimately familiar with the districts in which they lived and having regular opportunities of communicating with the great bulk of the population. In addition, of course, they could exercise the personal influence which came with their spiritual office, and their importance in local affairs. At the same time it seems clear that their prominence in successive political agitations depended less on their ability to dictate the opinions or actions of their congregations than on their unique suitability for the role of local agents and organisers. This became clear on those occasions when priests chose to support unpopular individuals or movements, or to oppose popular ones. As WHYTE (1960) puts it: 'on the whole . . . the Irish clergy could lead their people only in the direction that they wanted to go. The priests appeared all powerful so long as their views coincided with those of the electors; but their influence dropped almost to nothing if they took a line of their own'.

The limits of clerical authority were even more clearly revealed in the case of political violence. Here traditional Catholic theology, a general conservatism and fear of the possible repercussions both for the church and for its members, dictated a policy of firm opposition. The impact of that opposition was inevitably somewhat diluted by the willingness of a small minority of dissident priests to offer sympathy and active support to revolutionary movements. In addition, as O'SHEA has shown, the Catholic clergy of the later nineteenth century shared in the general ambivalence which allowed men of violence, once dead or superannuated, to be widely seen as objects of sympathy and even admiration. Where active revolutionary or conspiratorial movements were concerned, however, the attitude of the overwhelming majority of Catholic clergy was clear. The Defenders and United Irishmen in the 1790s, the Ribbonmen and agrarian secret societies of the early and mid-nineteenth century, and the Fenians of the 1860s and after, were all denounced in pastorals and sermons and their members excluded from the sacraments or declared excommunicate. Yet neither condemnations nor spiritual sanctions appear to have been particularly effective in deterring Catholics from joining the movements concerned. In all of these cases, furthermore, the church was throwing its authority against movements which had the support only of a section of the population. The agrarian secret societies of the pre-Famine period were predominantly movements of the rural poor. Large farmers, employers of labour and lessors of small plots to the landless, were more likely to be their victims than their collaborators. In some cases, indeed, priests in disturbed areas organised their more 'respectable' parishioners into vigilante groups to assist in suppressing agrarian crime. In the case of the Fenians, similarly, the hostility of the Catholic clergy, as O'SHEA makes clear, was shared by the majority of their congregations, and in particular by the farming population. It was only at a much later stage, between 1919 and 1922, that bishops and priests confronted a movement committed to the use of political violence which had the support of a wide cross-section of the Catholic population. When this happened, it was the church which gave ground, in part by explicitly modifying its earlier uncompromising opposition to violent methods, in part by maintaining a discreet silence until the conflict had been won.

A crucial element in any assessment of the political role of the Catholic clergy concerns the social background from which its members were drawn. Supporters and critics alike attributed much of the exceptional influence which Irish priests seemed to exercise over their flocks to their relatively humble social origins. In particular it was argued that the establishment in 1795 of a seminary at Maynooth had created a body of priests drawn from the lower levels of the Catholic population, men who shared the prejudices and passions of their flocks and with whom their people could identify. This, however, was a gross exaggeration. Maynooth, in the first place, did not become the main supplier of priests to Irish dioceses anything like as quickly as has often been assumed. Even in 1853 only 53 per cent of all priests serving in Irish dioceses had been educated at the college. To study at Maynooth, furthermore, may have been somewhat less expensive than to attend a continental seminary — as prospective priests had been forced to do in the eighteenth century — but a training there was by no means cheap. The expense of maintaining a student at the college, the fees charged to those who were not nominated to one of the free places available, and the cost of educating a youth to the standard required for entry into the college added up to a substantial investment. As a result the great majority of Maynooth priests, like those trained elsewhere in Ireland or abroad, were the sons of substantial tenant farmers or of the lower middle and middle classes of the towns and cities. Nor was it true, as contemporaries alleged, that it was graduates of Maynooth who were primarily responsible for the new role of the Catholic clergy as leaders of popular agitations. O'FERRALL's study of Co. Longford in the 1820s, and O'SHEA's account of Co. Tipperary in the decades after the Famine, both confirm that Maynooth-educated priests were neither more active nor more radical in their politics than those trained at other seminaries.

On the broader question of the importance of the relatively humble social origins of the Catholic clergy, contemporary claims must also be assessed with caution, at least where the first half of the nineteenth century is concerned. A variety of recent studies have drawn attention to the differences in circumstances and outlook that separated the farming class of pre-Famine Ireland form the much larger group of rural poor, the labourers, cottiers and occupiers of small holdings. Against such a background, the Catholic clergy, sons for the most part of medium and larger farmers, must be seen as drawn from a relatively favoured stratum within Catholic rural society, and it would be unwise to attribute too much to a solidarity between priests and people based on common social origins. In the second half of the century, however, all this changed. The Famine, and the continued heavy emigration of the decades that followed, transformed the social structure of rural Ireland, sweeping away large numbers of the rural poor while leaving the farming population relatively untouched. As the tenant farmer became increasingly the dominant figure in the Irish countryside, the potential for a close identification between priests and people increased. Equally important, these changes in class structure transformed the nature of rural social conflict. In the first half of the nineteenth century, as already mentioned, agrarian violence was in many cases a result of conflicts between farmers and the rural poor. After the Famine, as cottiers largely disappeared from the Irish countryside, and the labourers dwindled into a depressed minority, such tensions ceased to be of central importance. Instead the Catholic clergy were able to give their support or tacit approval to agitations which united the greater part of their congregations against external enemies, in the form of landlordism and the state, and whose demands for social change were of a kind which they could endorse without serious qualms.

A DEVOTIONAL REVOLUTION ?

Changes in ecclesiastical organisation and discipline, relations between members of different religious denominations, the interaction of religion and politics: all these are interesting and important questions. To complete the picture, however, it is also necessary to say something about religion itself. What did the doctrines and practices of the different churches mean to the ordinary men and women who made up their congregations, and how did that meaning change in the course of the nineteenth century?

Such questions, important to any historian of religion, have a particular relevance in the case of Ireland. To-day the single most striking feature distinguishing Ireland from the rest of Western Europe is the continued loyalty of the great majority of its inhabitants to institutional religion. In modern Austria, for example, around one-third of all Catholics attend religious services at least once a week. In urban Italy the figure is less than 30 per cent, while in France it has been estimated at only a little over one-fifth. In Ireland, on the other hand, a survey taken in 1972-3 found that 91 per cent of adult Catholics claimed to attend mass at least once a week, while almost one person in four claimed to attend more often. Where Irish Protestants are concerned, the contrast with comparable populations elsewhere is equally striking. In working-class Belfast, it is true, regular church attendance is confined to a minority: one estimate puts attendance among inhabitants of the Shankill district as low as 15 per cent. Even this, however, compares favourably with the level recorded in working-class communities in Great Britain. Outside working-class Belfast, meanwhile, the majority remain regular church attenders. In Northern Ireland to-day more than one-third of Protestants claim to attend church at least once a week, and almost two-thirds at least once a month: a level of attendance up to four times higher than that recorded in contemporary England or Sweden.[8] To what extent do the origins of these exceptionally high levels of popular devotion, among both Catholics and Protestants, lie in the nineteenth century?

Where Irish Protestants are concerned, the early and mid-nineteenth century saw major changes in religious attitudes and behaviour. Reports on parishes in Counties Antrim and Londonderry compiled for the Ordnance Survey in the 1830s noted a marked 'improvement' in the character of the population, reflected in increased church attendance, stricter observance of the Sabbath, and the decline of disreputable amusements such as cock-fighting, their place being taken by more decorous recreations, for example reading clubs and singing schools dedicated to sacred music. Although much of this change took place within the framework of the newly reinvigorated major denominations, the demand for a more vital and demanding form of religion was also reflected in the rapid growth of the lesser Protestant sects. The Baptists, for example, grew from around 500 members in 1800 to an estimated 2,000 by 1818 and to 4,237 by 1861. On a much larger scale, the number enrolled in Methodist societies rose from 3,000 in the late 1760s to 19,000 by 1800 and to 36,903 by 1830. Like its English counterpart, Irish Methodism appealed to popular audiences by offering satisfactions not found in the older-established churches: direct emotionally charged preaching, the psychological release offered by mutual confession of sins, a sense of companionship and shared commitment. Early Methodism had made progress in both north and south but its spectacular growth in the late eighteenth and early nineteenth centuries was achieved mainly in Ulster. In particular Methodism grew in areas where the Protestant population was predominantly Anglican: in south-west Ulster and in the linen-producing district centred on Co. Armagh. It made relatively little impact in the Presbyterian-dominated north-east. In Belfast, on the other hand, Methodism had a clear appeal to sections of the working class. By 1861 Methodists made up 4 per cent of the population of Belfast, and 3 per cent in both Co. Fermanagh and Co. Armagh, the highest proportions found anywhere in Ireland.

The character of this increase in religious fervour, and the reasons for it, have been the subject of some debate. GIBBON suggests a direct link between religious and economic change. The rationalistic brand of Christianity that had flourished among the independent farmers and weavers of the late eighteenth and early nineteenth centuries was progressively displaced by a new type of popular religion, enthusiastic, fundamentalist and deeply emotional, that better satisfied the psychological needs of a proletarianised work force. The first part of this analysis has been effectively challenged by MILLER (1978), who points, for example, to the prominent part played by millenarian prophecies in the United Irish movement of the 1790s as evidence that the religious culture of the farmers and weavers of the north-east can hardly have been of the temperate, rationalist character suggested by GIBBON. Instead, MILLER suggests, the transition was from one variety of evangelicalism, 'prophetic', to another, 'conversionist', as a 'modernisation' of attitudes restricted the domain within which the miraculous could be seen as operating from the external world to the individual psyche. This, however, is to interpret contemporary religious doctrine rather literally. Although GIBBON may have exaggerated the influence of Enlightenment ideas among lower-class Presbyterians in the later eighteenth century, he is surely correct in seeing the subsequent growth of enthusiastic religion, among Presbyterians and others, primarily as a response to new emotional and psychological needs. Thus HEMPTON (1986) emphasises the connection between the growth of Ulster Methodism and the political and sectarian tensions of the early nineteenth century. One of the most spectacular surges in Methodist growth, for example, came in 1799-1802, the years immediately following the rebellion of 1798. Secondly, and probably even more important, there were the rapid economic changes of the early and mid-nineteenth century: the rise and then decline of cotton manufacture, the collapse of domestic spinning and later domestic weaving, the agricultural depression of the post-war decades, the emergence of factory-based industry and of an industrial proletariat. To those threatened or disoriented by these changes, or enduring new and harsh conditions, an intense, doctrinally simple, emotionally-charged religion offered consolation, reassurance and psychological release. In addition, CONNOLLY (1983A) has suggested, evangelical religion may have played a role similar to that which has been attributed to it in England, providing the stimulus to self-discipline, and the alternative outlet for surplus energies, which helped men and women to adapt to a new and more restrictive work discipline.

The strength of the appeal of popular evangelicalism by the mid-nineteenth century was vividly revealed in the religious revival of 1859. Sparked off by news of a wave of religious enthusiasm sweeping the eastern half of the United States, this movement began in mid-Antrim towards the end of 1858, spreading rapidly across the greater part of Ulster during the following summer. A total of 100,000 persons was reported to have been converted, including Protestants of all denominations and also, it was claimed, numbers of Catholics. In theory the revival consisted of individual conversions, in which those affected found themselves smitten by an overwhelming recognition of their sinfulness, then comforted and inspired by a conviction that those sins had been forgiven. In practice, the rapid spread of the movement clearly depended on the seizure of whole communities by a powerful wave of collective emotion. At the Raceview Woollen Mills in Broughshane, Co. Antrim, for example, it was discovered after the breakfast-time break on the morning of Saturday, 21 May, that six or seven of the operatives were so afflicted by distress of soul that they could not return to work. By noon the excitement had become so general that the factory had to close, and when work resumed on the Monday morning nearly half the employees were still absent in the throes of conversion. The anguished interval between the first awful realisation of personal sinfulness and the surge of confidence in salvation through God's grace — a period lasting hours and sometimes days — was in many cases accompanied by a range of physical manifestations. The more exotic of these, as with the young ladies of Belfast who woke from sleep to find the words 'Jesus Christ' imprinted on their breasts, were disowned by the sponsors of the revival, but others were accepted as genuine. The Rev. S. J. Moore of Ballymena, a strong supporter of the movement, described how many of those smitten by a sense of sin 'fall as nerveless and paralysed, and powerless, as if killed instantly by a gun shot. . . The whole frame trembles as like an aspen leaf, an intolerable weight is felt upon the chest, a choking sensation is experienced and relief from this found only in the loud, urgent prayer for deliverance'.[9] In Coleraine, where it was claimed that one-fifth of the town's population was converted, the newly-erected Town Hall was opened as a hospital where those unbearably stricken could find refuge and help as they awaited the coming of peace.

The events of 1859, despite their spectacular character, cannot be seen in isolation. They followed several decades of growing popular religious enthusiasm and also, as BROOKE points out, the conversion of the Synod of Ulster over the preceding twenty years to a revivalist theology. Where the long term significance of the revival is concerned, supporters claimed that its practical effects were immediately apparent in increased church attendance, in a sharp decline in crime and drunkenness, and in a general improvement in morals. But the impact on individual lives of this one period of intense collective emotion was often short-lived. Among the Baptists of Tobermore, analysed by KINGDON, membership, which had already grown during the 1850s, rose sharply during 1859-60, but by 1874 had fallen back to the levels of 1849-50. In 1874-5, on the other hand, further efforts by the Irish Evangelisation Society once again brought an increase in membership, this time with more permanent effect. Elsewhere too revivalist efforts continued in the years after 1859. The American evangelists Moody and Sankey, for example, visited Ulster four times between 1867 and 1892. The smaller Protestant denominations continued to expand, the number of Baptists rising from 4,237 in 1861 to 7,062 by 1901, the number of Methodists from 45,399 to 62,006. Their growth at a time of overall decline of population, along with the proliferation of gospel halls unattached to any denomination, were further evidence of the continuing demand for vital preaching and intense emotional experience.

The emergence and spread of a new variety of popular religion, characterised by a fundamentalist theology and by an emphasis on personal experience, and the accompanying loss by the two major denominations of their former near-monopoly of religious life, were major developments in the history of nineteenth-century Protestantism. This does not mean that they necessarily affected all, or even a majority, of Protestants. Where denominational fragmentation is concerned, for example, it is important to remember that even in 1901 96 per cent of all Ulster Protestants were returned in the census as either Anglicans or Presbyterians. Some of these, it is true, would have found their most intense religious experiences, not in the churches to which they continued to give nominal allegiance, but in Gospel Halls or at revivalist meetings. At the same time it is clear that we also need to know a great deal more about those Protestants who remained attached to institutional religion of a traditional variety. We also need to know more about those who were indifferent to religion of any kind. Studies of nineteenth-century Britain have pointed to the existence of two separate working class cultures, 'respectable' and 'rough', focussed on the alternative centres of the chapel and the pub. GRAY's account of the changing character of popular entertainment in Belfast, where the emergence of a new style of respectable working-class recreation took place side by side with a continuing tradition of bawdiness and heavy drinking, suggests that a similar distinction existed there and probably in other industrial centres in Ulster. Here too more detailed exploration will be needed before it becomes possible to attempt an estimate of the real strength of Protestantism. However S. E. GRIBBON, in an admittedly impressionistic survey, concludes that already by the beginning of the twentieth century the level of religious commitment shown by all sections of the Protestant population of Belfast was markedly higher than that seen in contemporary England.

Among Irish Catholics too, the nineteenth century saw major changes in religious attitudes and behaviour. At the beginning of the century the religious practice of a large section of the population fell significantly short of the obligatory minimum prescribed by their church. The most concrete evidence for this lies in the detailed survey of church attendance carried out in 1834 by the Commissioners of Public Instruction. MILLER (1975), analysing the figures for selected parishes,

D

organises his results under three headings: rural parishes in which at least 25 per cent of the population were recorded in the census of 1851 as able to speak Irish, rural parishes in which the proportion of Irish speakers was less than 25 per cent, and towns. In the first type of parish, he concludes, attendance at mass on a normal Sunday accounted for between 20 and 40 per cent of the Catholic population. In the second, attendance ranged from 30 to 60 per cent. It was only in the towns, and in one rural area in Co. Wexford, that attendance levels of 70 per cent or more were recorded. These percentages, of course, relate to the total Catholic population. Some allowance must be made for young children, for those incapacitated by illness or old age, and for those prevented by inescapable domestic or other duties, all of whom would have been exempted from the obligation to attend Sunday mass. Even if these groups are estimated at a quarter of the total population, we are still left with a sizable group — in some parishes more than half the inhabitants — who were obliged to attend mass but did not do so. Some may have been kept away by lack of church accommodation, or because they lived too far from a Catholic place of worship for attendance to be practicable. But MILLER is able to cite cases in which neither of these considerations can be made to explain the absence from Sunday mass of a substantial proportion of the able-bodied adult population.

Other aspects of Catholic religious practice do not lend themselves to precise quantitative treatment of the same kind. But there is nevertheless much evidence to suggest that there too popular practice was restricted in both range and frequency. Thus there were frequent complaints that large numbers failed to perform their 'Easter duty' by confessing and receiving communion at least once annually, at or around Easter. Even where that strict obligation was fulfilled, it appears to have been unusual to confess or receive communion more than two or three times a year at most. Large numbers reached adulthood without having been confirmed, and it is likely that some were never confirmed at all. Non-obligatory religious services, such as benediction and stations of the cross, were unknown in many parishes and common only in a few. An Austrian Redemptorist, carrying out a mission in Enniskillen in 1852, discovered that the people there 'had never even witnessed benediction of the Blessed Sacrament, never seen incense rise from a thurible'.[10] The physical circumstances of Catholic worship were in most cases unimpressive, providing little scope for the external display which comprises an important feature of modern Catholic liturgy. Churches were in general plain, sparsely furnished structures, largely bare of ornament. Vestments and altar furnishings were often shabby and ill-cared for and the use of candles, incense, music and devotional images was rare outside the larger towns and a few other areas of advanced liturgical development.

To say that Irish Catholics in the first half of the nineteenth century had only a limited participation in the formal observances of their church is not to suggest that they were indifferent to religion. On the contrary, observers frequently commented on the degree of religious devotion exhibited by the Catholic lower orders. What they were devoted to, however, was a popular religion, diverging from orthodox Catholicism in a range of important respects. Thus Irish Catholics were deeply attached to the rites of passage provided by their church: virtually all children were baptised, and to die without having received extreme unction at the hands of a priest was generally regarded as a calamity. To be married by a priest, equally, was regarded as important, although ecclesiastical regulations on consanguinity were held in little respect. Other rituals, however — Sunday mass, confession and communion other than at the point of death — were considered less significant. At least as important, and possibly more so, were a range of beliefs and observances only partly or not at all sanctioned by the church authorities. Prominent among these was the celebration of certain festivals marking turning points in the agricultural year, for example St Brigid's day (1 February), when crosses were woven from rushes and hung in the house and farm buildings to provide protection for the coming year, or May Eve and St John's Eve (23 June), both marked by the lighting of bonfires which became the focus both for protective rituals and for boisterous celebration. A similar combination of ceremonial and festive elements was seen in the patterns, held at a holy well or other sacred site on the feast day of the saint to whom that site was supposedly dedicated. There was also a whole range of lesser beliefs and practices: lucky and unlucky actions, charms which could be used to find lost objects, to heal an illness or to verify a dubious statement, and various methods of inflicting harm on others or of protecting oneself against supernatural aggression. The relationship between such beliefs and official Catholic doctrine was a complex one. In some cases popular magic had been partly Christianised, as when the ancient spring festival of Imbolc had been translated into the feast of St Brigid, or when observances at sacred springs had evolved into pilgrimages to the shrine of a patron saint. In others, for example the rituals surrounding May day or the harvest festival of Lughnasa, magical beliefs retained an independent existence, largely untouched by Christian symbolism or doctrine. In other cases again, Catholic emblems and rituals were reinterpreted in magical terms: prayers were incorporated into protective charms, blessings and other rituals were seen as having a magical efficacy, and priests were credited with supernatural powers. The strength of magical beliefs, and the fusion of Christian and non-Christian elements, were vividly revealed in the events of 9-15 June 1832, when reports that the Virgin Mary had appeared in person to distribute tokens that would provide protection against the approaching cholera epidemic detonated a spectacular panic, affecting thousands of people in three-quarters of the counties of Ireland.*

---

* Magic means the attempted manipulation of the supernatural for immediate practical purposes. As such it can in theory be distinguished from religion, which offers a general explanation of the meaning of human life, and whose rituals are symbolic rather than instrumental in purpose. In practice, however, this distinction is often difficult to uphold. On the one hand, religious rituals have commonly been credited with a practical efficacy, and religious believers have often had at best a limited awareness of the overall framework of ideas within which specific injunctions and prohibitions are located. On the other, it has been argued that the practices of popular magic in many cases rested on their own wider system of assumptions and explanations, and had a symbolic as well as a practical intent. Some writers have objected to the use of the term 'magic' at all, on the grounds that it is a pejorative label, uncritically accepting the judgement of contemporary elites, who institutionalised one set of beliefs as 'religion', while condemning all others as 'magic'. For an argument along these lines see Hildred Geertz, 'An Anthropology of Religion and Magic', *Journal of Interdisciplinary History*, VI, 1 (1975), 71-89; for a defence of the term see the reply by Keith Thomas, ibid. 91-109.

The picture of popular beliefs and attitudes which thus emerges—however it might be received in Ireland—is one familiar from studies of comparable rural societies at this time and earlier. Religious obligations were conceived of in contractual terms, as a means of placating or winning over unseen forces by means of adherence to a set of more or less arbitrary rules, rather than as a body of internalised values and attitudes. Religious practice was instrumental in character, seen as a means of achieving certain concrete ends. The intertwining of religious and magical elements reflected, not simple ignorance or backwardness, but a need for direct assistance and reassurance of a kind which religion alone could not provide. In a society where individual lives were critically affected by apparently random developments in weather, the yield of crops, the health of people and animals, magic provided a means of coming to terms with, and to some extent controlling, what would otherwise be a purely arbitrary pattern of good and bad fortune. In addition, popular religion had a strong communal and festive element. Patterns and similar gatherings brought neighbours together in a combination of celebration and protective ritual and provided the occasion for a general escape from a frugal and uneventful daily round. Even the violence which was a regular feature of such gatherings had its place, providing for the controlled release of what might otherwise have become dangerously disruptive energies and frustrations.

The extent to which popular beliefs and practices diverged from official Catholic doctrine and ritual varied according to a predictable regional and social pattern. Orthodox religious practice, as MILLER's figures make clear, was markedly stronger in the towns than in the countryside. The same distinction between urban and rural emerges from KEARNEY's account of the dual nature of Father Mathew's temperance crusade of 1838-45. In the countryside, this was a revivalist movement incorporating strong magical elements. In the towns, by contrast, it was a movement of popular self-improvement under middle-class patronage, promoting the values of thrift, industry and discipline, and linked to the world of O'Connellite politics rather than to that of traditional belief and custom. In rural areas, the hold of official religion was clearly greater in economically advanced and anglicised districts than in less prosperous areas where traditional culture remained strong. Within particular districts, finally, it seems clear that it was the poorer classes whose outlook and practice diverged most from those of official Catholicism. Mary Fogarty, growing up in Co. Limerick in the 1860s and '70s, recalled that the maids employed in her father's household did not involve themselves in the world of Catholic religious doctrine

> in the way we did who knew more about it. Although they were thankful
> for holy days and went to mass, they were really more interested in an
> old Irish world where fairies, witches and banshees took the place of
> our angels and saints.[11]

The gap between the beliefs and attitudes of official Catholicism and those of a large section of the population was further revealed in the efforts of the church authorities of the late eighteenth and early nineteenth centuries to suppress or reform a large part of popular custom. Traditional festivals such as the celebration of St John's Eve and the patterns held at holy wells, the festive wakes held over the bodies of the recently dead, road-side dances and other assemblies for amusement, were all denounced as occasions of drunkenness, brawling, idleness and sexual immorality. In addition unorthodox supernatural beliefs and rituals were condemned as superstitious or impious. Some of these matters, for example practices at wakes and holy wells, had been a cause of concern for centuries. At the same time it seems clear that the decades preceding the Famine saw a mounting attack on the culture of the Catholic poor. This development can in part be attributed to the changes which had taken place within the Irish church: as the clergy themselves became more disciplined, better organised and more zealous, so they became more anxious to improve the morals of their flocks. At the same time the assault on popular culture also reflected wider social changes. By the early nineteenth century growing literacy, rising standards of living, and exposure to outside influences had begun to undermine attachment to traditional attitudes and customs. This was particularly so among the more prosperous sections of the rural population, the group from

whose ranks the Catholic priesthood was overwhelmingly
recruited. In addition the superior education of the clergy, and
the growing status accorded them within Irish society, made
them particularly anxious to distance themselves from the less
sophisticated elements in their religious heritage, and to aspire
to new models of respectability. William Wilde, writing in 1849,
quoted the opinion of 'one of our most learned and observant
Roman Catholic friends': 'the tone of society in Ireland is
becoming more and more "*Protestant*" every year; the literature
is a Protestant one and even the priests are becoming more
Protestant in their conversation and manners'.[12]

These attempts to reshape the religious and moral life of
the Catholic population met with only limited success. By the
1830s and 1840s observers like Wilde had begun to comment,
with varying degrees of regret or approval, on the decline which
was taking place in popular amusements, in the celebration of
traditional festivals, and in the attention paid to magical beliefs
and rituals. Most agreed that the influence of the Catholic clergy
had been a factor, though by no means the only one, in that
decline. By the same period the range and quality of pastoral
services had been improved, as part of the general tightening
of ecclesiastical discipline. Preaching had become more
common, provision had been made — with the aid of lay assistants
recruited through the Confraternity of the Christian Doctrine —
for more systematic religious instruction of the young, religious
services were more frequent and more carefully conducted, and
there had been some development of devotional societies and
confraternities. In all of these respects, however, progress was
slow and uneven. In the mid-1830s, as the evidence of the
Commissioners of Public Instruction makes clear, only half or
less of the Catholic population met even the minimum obligatory
level of religious practice laid down by their church. In many
respects, indeed, the gap between official and popular
Catholicism probably widened rather than narrowed in the first
half of the nineteenth century. On the one hand the clergy, as
already seen, were becoming increasingly sophisticated in their
religious outlook. On the other the continued increase in population, from around 4.5 million in 1791 to 8.1 million by 1841,

swelled the ranks of the rural poor, the group which was least capable of contributing to the support of a church establishment and among whom the influence of official Catholicism was weakest.

What changed all this was the impact of the Great Famine. Deaths from fever and starvation, and migration during and after the Famine, drastically reduced the numbers of the rural poor, while leaving the farming class intact and even slightly strengthened. The contrast with the pre-Famine period was further heightened by the long period of high agricultural prices and general prosperity which began in the 1850s and continued up to the mid-1870s. As a result, the Catholic church, itself emerging from a period of internal reform and renewal, was left with a smaller but more prosperous population, which was both better able to support an ecclesiastical establishment adequate to its needs and more orthodox in its religious outlook. It was these developments which made possible the major reshaping of popular religious practice which LARKIN (1972) has called 'the devotional revolution'. In the two or three decades after the Famine, LARKIN suggests, attendance at Sunday mass for the first time became almost universal, while confession and communion became more regular and more frequent. The same period saw the widespread dissemination of a range of auxiliary services — benediction, stations of the cross, novenas, processions and retreats — as well as the routine use of scapulars, medals, religious images and other aids to private devotion. Individual religious practice was encouraged and regimented through the proliferation of lay confraternities and sodalities. Meanwhile the psychological impact of Catholic religious worship was increased by a transformation of its physical setting, as new or improved church buildings, more elaborate vestments and lavish altar furnishings allowed services to be conducted with a new emphasis on external magnificence and display. By all of these means, LARKIN suggests, 'the great mass of the Irish people became practicing Catholics, which they have uniquely and essentially remained both at home and abroad down to the present day'.

The changed environment in which the Catholic church operated in the decade after the Famine was reflected, not just in the transformation of religious practice, but also in the type of social discipline which it now became possible to maintain. Where the clergy of the early nineteenth century had struggled to transform a vigorous popular culture rooted in the life-style of the rural poor, their successors faced a more affluent Catholic laity, itself aspiring to new models of respectability, and hence more receptive to the imposition of a strict social discipline. By the end of the nineteenth century most of the aspects of Irish social life which had earlier been a cause of major concern to the church authorities — wakes, patterns, recreational violence, the various forms of popular magic — had disappeared or greatly declined. The close coincidence of clerical and lay standards of behaviour was clearly revealed in the case of sexual attitudes. The Catholic clergy of the late nineteenth century and after were to become notorious for the rigid sexual morality which they imposed on their congregations. In this, however, they only reflected the attitudes of the laity themselves, in a society where rigid patterns of inheritance, combined with a demographic regime that demanded that large numbers of men and women married only very late or not at all, made a very strict code of sexual behaviour essential. The tyranny which the clergy seemed to exercise over the sexual lives of their flocks may be set against their much more circumspect approach to the other major problem of social discipline to concern them in this period, that of drink. Thus MALCOLM has shown how the church authorities throughout the nineteenth century carefully kept their distance from movements of total abstinence. They did so partly because such movements were in general dominated by Protestants, but also because they recognised that to throw their influence behind a campaign for such a radical change in social habits would only weaken their authority. This explains why the Pioneer Total Abstinence Association, in which renunciation of alcohol became an act of religious devotion by a heroic few, rather than the desired behaviour of a whole nation, received a degree of official approval that had been withheld from its predecessors.

The suggestion that the Famine marked a central turning point in the development of Irish Catholicism, and in the relationship between church and people, has been challenged

E

in a major recent study. In *The Catholic Church in Nineteenth-Century Ireland: A Sociological Study*, Desmond Keenan has offered an explicit critique of the views of Larkin and Miller. The Catholic church of the first half of the nineteenth century was not, he suggests, hindered by any serious lack of resources, and it did not undergo a process of internal reform. Nor was there any great change in popular religious practice. Instead, Keenan argues, the various elements which Larkin presents as new developments of the period after the Famine can already be discovered in the first half of the nineteenth century. There were, he concedes, certain changes in the character of Irish Catholicism in the course of the century, but these were of a secondary nature: the creation of distinctively Catholic institutions and of a distinctively Catholic style of public worship, and the cultivation of a new emotionalism in spiritual matters. Even here, furthermore, the major developments came in the first half of the nineteenth century. The period between 1800 and 1850 was one of 'innovation', that between 1850 and 1900 merely of 'consolidation'.

To support these views, Keenan brings together a mass of detail, drawn from an impressively wide range of ecclesiastical archives. In some respects, he undoubtedly provides a corrective to earlier accounts. For example, he demonstrates effectively that the period of greatest activity in church building during the nineteenth century came in the years 1820-40, rather than—as Connolly (1982) and others had suggested—in the decades after the Famine. Where his overall analysis is concerned, however, two points must be made. The first is that his lengthy catalogues of the achievements of the early nineteenth century—schools founded, charitable organisations established, religious orders introduced or extended—fails consistently to recognise that, at a time of rapidly rising population, the Catholic church had to make considerable progress simply to maintain existing standards. To take a simple example: between 1800 and 1840 the number of parish priests and curates serving in Ireland increased by no less than 35 per cent, a major mobilisation of resources and a most impressive achievement. In the same period, however, the population of Ireland rose by over 50 per

cent, so that the number of Catholics for each parish priest or
curate actually increased, from around 2,700 to almost 3,000.
The superficially impressive rise in clerical numbers, in other
words, conceals an actual decline in the level of pastoral
services available to the laity.

The second major weakness of KEENAN's study is that it
seriously misrepresents the views it purports to refute. Neither
LARKIN nor MILLER denied that the changes they presented
as taking place in the decades after the Famine were fore-
shadowed by developments in the first half of the century. A
central element in LARKIN's argument was the completion
during the early nineteenth century of a substantial measure
of ecclesiastical reform, leaving the Catholic Church well
prepared to take advantage of the novel opportunities presented
by the changed conditions of post-Famine Ireland. He also drew
attention to the evidence, before the Famine, of 'a small but
perceptible change and increase in devotional practices',
affecting the minority of better-off, 'respectable' Catholics. In
the same way MILLER noted the existence of parishes in which
the level of church attendance in 1834 was more or less
comparable with those observed to-day. These, however, were
confined to the towns and — in MILLER's sample of parishes — to
one particularly prosperous area in Co. Wexford. Yet it is
precisely from such areas — from towns, from some dioceses in
the east of the country, most of all from the city and diocese
of Dublin — that the great bulk of KEENAN's evidence comes.
As for his insistence that it was the years 1800-1850 that marked
the period of 'innovation', it is necessary to distinguish between
institutional form and social reality. Thus, in the archdiocese
of Cashel, a Confraternity of the Blessed Sacrament, intended
to encourage more frequent confession and communion among
the laity, was set up as early as 1778. Yet in the part of that
diocese examined in TIERNEY's pioneering study, the parish
of Murroe and Boher, the Confraternity as late as 1852 had
only about 100 members in a population of over 5,000. Moreover
there were still at that point only two Sunday masses celebrated
in the parish. The 'innovation' may indeed have come in the
1770s. But the really important development was surely the

extension of a pattern of more frequent and more regular religious practice from a pious minority to the population as a whole. And this, it seems clear, took place only in the 1850s or later.

To say this is not to suggest that the last word has been said on the subject of Catholic religious practice in the first half of the nineteenth century. On the contrary, a great deal of work remains to be done. Thus KERR, in a short but penetrating discussion of the state of the Catholic church in the 1840s, uses visitation records from rural parts of the diocese of Dublin, and from the diocese of Cashel, to show that by this time the clergy of both dioceses appear to have been reasonably satisfied with the religious practice, and the general moral conduct, of their congregations. Once again, of course, this is evidence from areas in which one would expect the church of the pre-Famine period to have been better organised, and religious practice more highly developed, than average. At the same time the reports cited by KERR do suggest that the 'small but perceptible' increase in popular piety which LARKIN detected in the decades preceding the Famine may in fact have affected a larger section of the population than he and others have implied. Further evidence of the same kind may well lead to a greater emphasis on the pre-Famine origins of the 'devotional revolution', and on the role of the Famine — in this as in other matters — as an accelerator rather than the initiator of change.

How did the development of popular religion in nineteenth-century Ireland compare with what was seen in other parts of Europe at the same time? The answer is often given in the form of a stark contrast: in Ireland, attachment to organised religion survived and even grew, while elsewhere it declined catastrophically. But this is an oversimplification. The nineteenth century was not in fact a period of unqualified religious decline. Instead rapid social change and intensified social conflict produced contradictory results; they undermined the claims of official churches to represent whole societies, but at the same time gave religion a new role as part of the distinctive identity of particular groups or classes. As a result the nineteenth century was, in McLEOD's words, 'the archetypal period of secularisation, and a great age of religious revival'. In rural areas in particular, a process of 'Christianisation' or 'rechristianisation' continued in some cases into the second half of the nineteenth century. By the end of the period, it is true, adherence to organised religion had declined drastically among most urban populations and in some rural ones. There were other rural areas, however, in which high levels of religious practice continued up to the 1950s and '60s. Attachment to the churches also remained strong in those areas, urban and rural, in which the pressures of political and social conflict tended to reinforce rather than undermine religious loyalties. This was the case, for example, among the minority Catholic populations of the Netherlands and parts of northern Germany, and among Flemish speakers in parts of France and Belgium. It was even more strikingly so further east, among the Catholics of Poland.

The relevance of all this to Ireland is fairly clear. The Irish Catholic church, as its supporters never tired of pointing out, drew much of its popularity from its political independence. Its clergy, though counting few of the poor among their number, were not drawn from the social elite, and it had no formal links with the political establishment. The Protestant churches did of course have such links, but in the particular political circumstances of nineteenth-century Ireland this was unlikely to damage them in the eyes of even their most deprived members. Nor was adherence to the different churches weakened by political and social divisions within their membership. Elsewhere, and particularly in Catholic Europe, it was increasingly the conservative sections of the middle and upper classes who attended church regularly, while the radical bourgeoisie and the working class (or at least their menfolk) stayed away. In Ireland, on the other hand, the domination of politics by nationalist and sectarian issues muffled potential class conflict. Successive political movements, both Nationalist and Loyalist, drew support from all social classes, successfully urging the submersion of sectional interests in the service of common goals. In this process the churches, and in particular the Catholic church, were both important auxiliaries and the major ultimate beneficiaries.

If the religious revival of the nineteenth century was partly a response to social cleavage, it was also in part a response to uncomfortably rapid change. In an age when unprecedented economic advance disrupted traditional ways of life, many found in religion a symbol of continuity, order, and identity. Here too Ireland can be seen as an extreme example of a wider trend. Ireland, outside its north-east corner, may not have been directly affected as other regions were by the twin processes of industrialisation and urbanisation. But the pace of cultural change had nevertheless been rapid. By the middle of the nineteenth century, LARKIN suggests, Irish Catholics were affected by an 'identity crisis' arising out of the disappearance of the greater part of their traditional culture. For them the devotional revolution provided 'a substitute symbolic language and offered them a new cultural heritage with which they could identify and through which they could identify with one another'. From this point of view the development of Irish Catholicism presents one more example of a wider process described by CULLEN; he has suggested that Irish society experienced belated and therefore unusually rapid social change in recent centuries, which has stripped it of most of its traditions, and as a consequence artificial symbols of identity have had to be created to replace them. As in other areas of Irish life, furthermore, the inventions of the present were validated by a rewriting of the past. In particular, the real history of Irish Catholicism, with its complex interaction of popular and official traditions, was obscured beneath a legend of long-suffering but unwavering piety which it is only now becoming possible to dismantle.

NOTES

[1] This estimate is based partly on census statistics, and partly on unpublished work by David Dickson. See CONNOLLY (1982), pp. 27-8 for details.

[2] *Census of Ireland, 1861*, Part IV (Brit. Parl. Papers, 1863, LIX), p. 8.

[3] Quoted in AKENSON, p. 30.

[4] Michael MacDonagh, *The Viceroy's Post-Bag* (London, 1904), p. 99.

[5] *Observer*, quoted in *Dublin Evening Post*, 25 July 1822.

[6] Sir Richard Musgrave, quoted in W. E. H. Leckey, *A History of Ireland in the Eighteenth Century* (London, 1892), IV, 416.

[7] W. J. O'Neill Daunt, *Personal Recollections of the Late Daniel O'Connell, M.P.* (London, 1848), II, 7. James Dickey was in fact one of the leaders of the United Irish rebellion in County Antrim.

[8] For religious practice among Catholics see Maire Nic Giolla Phadraigh, 'Religion in Ireland: Preliminary Analysis', *Social Studies*, V, 2 (1976), 113-80. For Protestants see MILLER (1978), 89, n.81; John Hickey, *Religion and the Northern Ireland Problem* (Dublin, 1984), p. 129.

[9] Quoted in Carson, *God's River in Spate*, p. 104. For fraudulent manifestations see ibid. pp. 76-7; J. B. Armour, quoted in Public Record Office of Northern Ireland, *Report of the Deputy Keeper of the Records for the Years 1960-65* (1968), p. 53.

[10] E. Hosp, 'Redemptorist Mission in Enniskillen 1852', *Clogher Record*, VIII, 3 (1975), 268-70.

[11] Mary Carbery, *The Farm by Lough Gur: The Story of Mary Fogarty* (Cork, 1973), pp. 157-8.

[12] W. R. Wilde, *Irish Popular Superstitions* (Dublin, 1852), p. 17 fn.

SELECT BIBLIOGRAPHY

Religion pervaded so many aspects of life in nineteenth-century Ireland that a full bibliography is impracticable. The list offered here identifies major works relating to the principal topics touched on, including all items referred to in the text. For a more comprehensive bibliography see the relevant chapters of T. W. Moody (ed.), *Irish Historiography 1936-70* (Dublin, 1971) and Joseph Lee (ed.), *Irish Historiography 1970-79* (Cork, 1981). For the Catholic church see also J. J. Silke, 'The Roman Catholic Church in Ireland 1800-1922: A Survey of Recent Historiography', *Studia Hibernica*, XV (1975), 61-104.

The illusion of uniqueness has led to the history of religion in Ireland being all to often considered in misleading isolation. Hugh McLeod, *Religion and the People of Western Europe 1789-1970* (Oxford, 1981) is a superb synthesis whose major themes, as indicated above, do much to make developments in Ireland more intelligible. For useful comparisons with the picture of popular beliefs and practices that emerges from accounts of pre-Famine Catholicism see Marc Venard, 'Popular Religion in the Eighteenth Century', in W. J. Callahan and David Higgs (eds.), *Church and Society in Catholic Europe in the Eighteenth Century* (Cambridge, 1979), Olwen Hufton, 'The French Church', also in Callahan and Higgs (eds.), and Jean Delumeau, *Catholicism between Luther and Voltaire: A New View of the Counter Reformation* (London, 1977).

AKENSON, D. H. *The Church of Ireland: Ecclesiastical Reform and Revolution 1800-85* (New Haven, 1971).

————, *A Protestant in Purgatory: Richard Whately, Archbishop of Dublin* (Hamden, Conn. 1981).

BARKLEY, J. M. 'The Arian Schism in Ireland, 1830', in Derek BAKER (ed.), *Schism, Heresy and Religious Protest* (Cambridge, 1972), pp. 323-39.

BARTLETT, Thomas. 'An End to Moral Economy: The Irish Militia Disturbances of 1793', *Past and Present*, 99 (1983), 41-64—highlights the importance of the Catholic Relief Acts of 1792 and 1793 in accelerating the breakdown of relations between Catholics and Protestants.

BEW, Paul, and WRIGHT, Frank. 'The Agrarian Opposition in Ulster Politics 1848-87', in CLARK and DONNELLY (eds.), 192-229.

BOWEN, Desmond. *The Protestant Crusade in Ireland 1800-70: A Study of Protestant-Catholic Relations between the Act of Union and Disestablishment* (Dublin, 1978). The most complete account of the Second Reformation. Too narrowly focussed, however, to be a satisfactory account of 'Protestant-Catholic relations'.

————, *Paul Cardinal Cullen and the Shaping of Modern Irish Catholicism* (Dublin, 1983). A generally convincing portrayal of the man and his outlook. For its wider theses, see above, pp. 13, 26.

BROOKE, Peter. 'Religion and Secular Thought' in J. C. BECKETT et al., *Belfast: The Making of the City 1800-1914* (Belfast, 1983), pp. 111-28.

BRYNN, Edward. *The Church of Ireland in the Age of Catholic Emancipation* (New York, 1982)—primarily concerned with political aspects.

CARSON, John T. *God's River in Spate: The Story of the Religious Awakening of Ulster in 1859* (Belfast, 1958)—an uncritical and celebratory narrative, but one which has yet to be superseded by a proper historical study.

CLARK, Samuel and DONNELLY Jr., J. S. (eds.), *Irish Peasants: Violence and Political Unrest 1780-1914* (Madison, Wisconsin, 1983)—see articles by BEW and WRIGHT, DONNELLY and MILLER.

CONNELL, K. H. 'Catholicism and Marriage in the Century after the Famine', in *Irish Peasant Society: Four Historical Essays* (Oxford, 1968), 113-161—a pioneering study despite its uncritical, even reckless, approach to literary evidence in a particularly controversial area.

CONNOLLY, S. J. 'Catholicism in Ulster, 1800-1850', in Peter Roebuck (ed.), *Plantation to Partition: Essays in Ulster History in Honour of J. L. McCracken* (Belfast, 1981), 157-171.

————, *Priests and People in Pre-Famine Ireland 1780-1845* (Dublin, 1982).

————, 'Religion, Work Discipline and Economic Attitudes: The Case of Ireland', in T. M. DEVINE and David DICKSON (eds.), *Ireland and Scotland 1600-1850* (Edinburgh, 1983), 235-45.

————, 'The "Blessed Turf": Cholera and Popular Panic in Ireland, June 1832', *Irish Historical Studies*, XXIII, 91 (1983), 214-32.

CORISH, P. J. (ed.), *A History of Irish Catholicism.* These modest but invaluable sections of an uncompleted co-operative project are invariably thorough and reliable, and in many cases contain substantial original research. For the period considered here, see J. H. WHYTE, 'Political Problems 1850-60' and P. J. CORISH, 'Political Problems 1860-78', published together as Vol. V, parts 2 and 3 (Dublin, 1967); Ignatius MURPHY, 'Primary Education'; S. V. O SUILLEABHAIN, 'Secondary Education'; and Fergal McGRATH, 'University Education', published together as Vol. V, part 6 (Dublin, 1971); T. P. CUNNINGHAM, 'Church Reorganisation'; and T. P. KENNEDY, 'Church Building', published together as Vol. V, parts 7 and 8 (Dublin, 1970).

————, 'Gallicanism at Maynooth: Archbishop Cullen and the Royal Visitation of 1853', in Art COSGROVE and Donal McCARTNEY (eds.), *Studies in Irish History Presented to R. Dudley Edwards* (Dublin, 1979), 176-89.

————, 'The Catholic Community in the Nineteenth Century', *Archivium Hibernicum*, XXXVIII (1983), 26-33.

CULLEN, L. M. *The Emergence of Modern Ireland 1600-1900* (London, 1981)—important here both for its discussion of sectarian tensions in Co. Armagh (chap. 6, 9) and for its broader theme of the weakness of tradition in modern

Ireland and the consequent devotion to symbols of identity (see especially pp. 135-9, 254-6).

DONNELLY, J. S. 'Pastorini and Captain Rock: Millenarianism and Sectarianism in the Rockite Movement of 1821-4', in CLARK and DONNELLY (eds.), 102-139.

ELLIOTT, Marianne. *Partners in Revolution: The United Irishmen and France* (New Haven and London, 1982) — the most comprehensive recent treatment of popular politics and sectarian tensions in the crucial period 1791-1815.

EVERSLEY, D. E. C. 'The Demography of the Irish Quakers, 1650-1850', in J. M. GOLDSTROM and L. A. CLARKSON (eds.), *Irish Population, Economy and Society* (Oxford, 1981), pp. 57-88.

GIBBON, Peter. *The Origins of Ulster Unionism: The Formation of Popular Protestant Politics and Ideology in Nineteenth-Century Ireland* (Manchester, 1975).

GRAY, John. 'Popular Entertainment', in J. C. BECKETT et al., *Belfast: The Making of the City 1800-1914* (Belfast, 1983), pp. 99-110.

GRIBBON, H. D. 'Irish Baptists in the Nineteenth Century: Economic and Social Background', *Irish Baptist Hist. Soc. Jn.*, XVI (1983/4), 4-18.

GRIBBON, S. E. (as S. E. BAKER), 'Orange and Green: Belfast 1832-1912', in H. J. DYOS and Michael WOLFF (eds.), *The Victorian City: Images and Realities* (2 vols. London, 1973), II, 789-814.

— — — —, 'An Irish City: Belfast 1911', in David Harkness and Mary O'Dowd (eds.), *The Town in Ireland* (Belfast, 1981), pp. 203-220.

HAIRE, J. L. M. et al., *Challenge and Conflict: Essays in Irish Presbyterian History and Doctrine* (Antrim, 1981) — apart from HOLMES's essay, a disappointing collection.

HEMPTON, D. N. 'The Methodist Crusade in Ireland 1795-1845', *Irish Historical Studies*, XXII, 85 (1980), 33-48.

— — — —, 'Methodism in Irish Society 1770-1830', *Transactions of the Royal Historical Society* (forthcoming, 1986).

HEPBURN, A. C. 'Catholics in the North of Ireland, 1850-1921: The Urbanization of a Minority', in HEPBURN (ed.), *Minorities in History* (London, 1978), pp. 84-101; 'Work, Class and Religion in Belfast, 1871-1911', *Irish Economic and Social History*, X (1983), 33-50 — census-based studies, essential to any consideration of the relationship between religion and social structure in Ulster.

HOLMES, R. Finlay. *Henry Cooke* (Belfast, 1981). A lucid, impeccably argued dissection of a central figure, this is also, despite its modest tone, the best introduction for the non-specialist to the history of nineteenth-century Presbyterianism.

KEARNEY, H. F. 'Fr Mathew: Apostle of Modernisation', in Art COSGROVE and Donal McCARTNEY (eds.), *Studies in Irish History Presented to R. Dudley Edwards* (Dublin, 1979), 164-75.

KEENAN, Desmond. *The Catholic Church in Nineteenth-Century Ireland: A Sociological Study* (Dublin, 1983).

KENNEDY, Liam. 'The Roman Catholic Church and Economic Growth in Nineteenth-Century Ireland', *Economic and Social Review*, X, 1 (1978), 45-60.

————, 'The Early Response of the Irish Catholic Clergy to the Co-Operative Movement', *Irish Historical Studies*, XXI, 8 (1978), 55-74.

KERR, D. A. *Peel, Priests and Politics: Sir Robert Peel's Administration and the Roman Catholic Church in Ireland 1841-6* (Oxford, 1982) — primarily concerned with politics, but opening with a valuable survey of the state of the Catholic church in the 1840s.

KINGDON, D. P. 'Irish Baptists and the Revival of 1859 with Special Reference to Tobermore', *Irish Baptist Historical Society Journal*, I (1968/9), 19-30.

LARKIN, Emmet. *The Roman Catholic Church and the Creation of the Modern Irish State 1878-86* (Philadelphia and Dublin, 1975); *The Roman Catholic Church and the Plan of Campaign in Ireland, 1886-1888* (Cork, 1978); *The*

Roman Catholic Church and the Fall of Parnell 1888-91 (Liverpool, 1979)— detailed segments of old-fashioned political history, eccentrically presented as a 'mosaic' of extended quotation from archival sources, and largely ignoring other writing on the topics dealt with. *The Making of the Roman Catholic Church in Ireland 1850-60* (Chapel Hill, North Carolina, 1980) is somewhat better in the latter two respects, but still rather narrower in scope than its title suggests.

— — — — , 'Economic Growth, Capital Investment and the Roman Catholic Church in Nineteenth-Century Ireland', *American Historical Review*, LXXII (1967), 852-84; 'The Devotional Revolution in Ireland, 1850-75', ibid. LXXVII (1972); 'Church, State and Nation in Modern Ireland', ibid. LXXX (1975), all three reprinted, with some afterthoughts, in *The Historical Dimensions of Irish Catholicism* (New York, 1981)— three general articles outlining a comprehensive interpretation of the development of Irish Catholicism during the nineteenth century. The essential starting point for all subsequent discussion.

MacDonagh, Oliver. *Ireland* (Englewood Cliffs, New Jersey, 1968).

— — — — , 'The Politicization of the Irish Catholic Bishops, 1800-20', *Historical Journal*, XVIII (1975), 37-53.

McDowell, R. B. *The Church of Ireland 1869-1969* (London, 1975).

McMinn, 'Presbyterianism and Politics in Ulster, 1871-1906', *Studia Hibernica*, 21 (1981), 127-46.

Macaulay, Ambrose. *Dr Russell of Maynooth* (London, 1983)— elegant biography of a leading Catholic intellectual that casts useful sidelights on various aspects of ecclesiastical affairs.

Malcolm, Elizabeth. 'The Catholic Church and the Irish Temperance Movement 1838-1901', *Irish Historical Studies*, XXIII, 89 (1982), 1-16.

Miller, D. W. 'Irish Catholicism and the Great Famine', *Journal of Social History*, IX, 1 (1975), 81-98— includes the crucial analysis of church attendance statistics.

MILLER, D. W. 'Presbyterianism and "Modernisation" in Ulster', *Past and Present,* 80 (1978), 66-90.

— — — — , 'The Armagh Troubles 1784-95', in CLARK and DONNELLY (eds.), (1983) 155-91.

MURPHY, Ignatius. 'Some Attitudes to Religious Freedom and Ecumenism in Pre-Emancipation Ireland', *Irish Ecclesiastical Record,* CV (1966), 93-104.

NORMAN, E. R. R. *The Catholic Church and Ireland in the Age of Rebellion 1859-73* (London, 1965).

O'FERRALL, Fergus. ' "The Only Lever. . .": The Catholic Priest in Irish Politics, 1823-29', *Studies,* LXX, 280 (1981), 308-24.

O'SHEA, James. *Priest, Politics and Society in Post-Famine Ireland: A Study of County Tipperary 1850-1891* (Dublin, 1983).

Ó TUATHAIGH, Gearóid. 'Gaelic Ireland, Popular Politics and Daniel O'Connell', *Galway Archaeological and Historical Society Journal,* XXXIV (1974-5), 21-34.

REYNOLDS, J. A. *The Catholic Emancipation Crisis in Ireland 1823-29* (New Haven, 1954).

SENIOR, Hereward. *Orangeism in Ireland and Britain, 1795-1836* (London, 1966).

STEWART, A. T. Q. *The Narrow Ground: Aspects of Ulster 1609-1969* (London, 1977)—important mainly for its sober assessment of the limitations of Presbyterian radicalism even at its late eighteenth-century high point.

TIERNEY, Mark. *Murroe and Boher: The History of an Irish Country Parish* (Dublin, 1966)—pioneering local study, strikingly anticipating LARKIN's conclusions, six years later, regarding the existence of a 'devotional revolution'.

WHELAN, Kevin. 'The Catholic Parish, the Catholic Chapel and Village Development in Ireland', *Irish Geography,* XVI (1983), 1-15.

WHYTE, J. H. 'The influence of the Catholic Clergy on Elections in Nineteenth-Century Ireland', *English Historical Review,* LXXV (1960), 239-59.

— — — —, 'The Appointment of Catholic Bishops in Nineteenth-Century Ireland', *Catholic Historical Review,* XLVIII (1962), 12-32.

For Whyte (1967) see above under Corish (ed.).

WOODS, C. J. 'The General Election of 1892: The Catholic Clergy and the Defeat of the Parnellites', in F. S. L. LYONS and R. A. J. HAWKINS (eds.), *Ireland Under the Union: Varieties of Tension* (Oxford, 1980), 289-319.